Number 144
Winter 2014

New Directions for Evaluation

Paul R. Brandon
Editor-in-Chief

Needs Assessment: Trends and a View Toward the Future

James W. Altschuld
Ryan Watkins
Editors

NEEDS ASSESSMENT: TRENDS AND A VIEW TOWARD THE FUTURE
James W. Altschuld, Ryan Watkins (eds.)
New Directions for Evaluation, no. 144
Paul R. Brandon, Editor-in-Chief

Microfilm copies of issues and articles are available in 16mm and 35mm, as well as microfiche in 105mm, through University Microfilms Inc., 300 North Zeeb Road, Ann Arbor, MI 48106-1346.

New Directions for Evaluation is indexed in Academic Search Alumni Edition (EBSCO Publishing), Education Research Complete (EBSCO Publishing), Higher Education Abstracts (Claremont Graduate University), SCOPUS (Elsevier), Social Services Abstracts (ProQuest), Sociological Abstracts (ProQuest), Worldwide Political Science Abstracts (ProQuest).

NEW DIRECTIONS FOR EVALUATION (ISSN 1097-6736, electronic ISSN 1534-875X) is part of The Jossey-Bass Education Series and is published quarterly by Wiley Subscription Services, Inc., A Wiley Company, at Jossey-Bass, One Montgomery Street, Suite 1200, San Francisco, CA 94104-4594.

SUBSCRIPTIONS for individuals cost $89 for U.S./Canada/Mexico/international. For institutions, $358 U.S.; $398 Canada/Mexico; $432 international. Electronic only: $89 for individuals all regions; $358 for institutions all regions. Print and electronic: $98 for individuals in the U.S., Canada, and Mexico; $122 for individuals for the rest of the world; $430 for institutions in the U.S.; $470 for institutions in Canada and Mexico; $504 for institutions for the rest of the world.

EDITORIAL CORRESPONDENCE should be addressed to the Editor-in-Chief, Paul R. Brandon, University of Hawai'i at Mānoa, 1776 University Avenue, Castle Memorial Hall Rm 118, Honolulu, HI 96822-2463.

www.josseybass.com

Editorial Policy and Procedures

New Directions for Evaluation, a quarterly sourcebook, is an official publication of the American Evaluation Association. The journal publishes works on all aspects of evaluation, with an emphasis on presenting timely and thoughtful reflections on leading-edge issues of evaluation theory, practice, methods, the profession, and the organizational, cultural, and societal context within which evaluation occurs. Each issue of the journal is devoted to a single topic, with contributions solicited, organized, reviewed, and edited by one or more guest editors.

The editor-in-chief is seeking proposals for journal issues from around the globe about topics new to the journal (although topics discussed in the past can be revisited). A diversity of perspectives and creative bridges between evaluation and other disciplines, as well as chapters reporting original empirical research on evaluation, are encouraged. A wide range of topics and substantive domains is appropriate for publication, including evaluative endeavors other than program evaluation; however, the proposed topic must be of interest to a broad evaluation audience. For examples of the types of topics that have been successfully proposed, go to http://www.josseybass.com/WileyCDA/Section/id-155510.html.

Journal issues may take any of several forms. Typically they are presented as a series of related chapters, but they might also be presented as a debate; an account, with critique and commentary, of an exemplary evaluation; a feature-length article followed by brief critical commentaries; or perhaps another form proposed by guest editors.

Submitted proposals must follow the format found via the Association's website at http://www.eval.org/Publications/NDE.asp. Proposals are sent to members of the journal's Editorial Advisory Board and to relevant substantive experts for single-blind peer review. The process may result in acceptance, a recommendation to revise and resubmit, or rejection. The journal does not consider or publish unsolicited single manuscripts.

Before submitting proposals, all parties are asked to contact the editor-in-chief, who is committed to working constructively with potential guest editors to help them develop acceptable proposals. For additional information about the journal, see the "Statement of the Editor-in-Chief" in the Spring 2013 issue (No. 137).

Paul R. Brandon, Editor-in-Chief
University of Hawai'i at Mānoa
College of Education
1776 University Avenue
Castle Memorial Hall, Rm. 118
Honolulu, HI 968222463
e-mail: nde@eval.org

This issue of *New Directions for Evaluation* is dedicated to the memory of John Wedman (1949–2013)—a dear friend, a valued and respected colleague.

Contents

EDITORS' NOTES

H ave you ever wondered how (and why) two relatively normal
friends would ever take on editing a special issue of a journal or
a book together? Are you curious about how they come up with a
theme and then find authors? To give you some insights, below is a recre-
ation of a conversation that led up to this issue of *New Directions for Evaluation*. It may lead to questions about our sanity, but in the end hopefully
it will reflect what a wonderful opportunity it is to work closely with col-
leagues and how the process can work for those who may be considering
taking a similar journey in the future. At the same time, our "dramatized"
conversation illustrates why we wanted the chapters that you now find in
this issue and what we hope they will contribute to the professional field.

A conversation between Jim Altschuld (JA) and Ryan Watkins (RW)
about an issue of *New Directions for Evaluation* on needs assessment (over
lunch, at the 2012 AEA conference in Minneapolis):

> Ryan, I think that we should do an issue of *New Directions* devoted to the
> current state of needs assessment and what is emergent in the field. I don't
> think that there has been one on the topic before and a lot is going on now.
> The timing seems good to me and we ought to do it. As I have threatened
> many times before, I am retired and this might be my last AEA conference.

Question from RW:

> Yeah, right Jim. We will be having lunch at the 2020 conference (in Hon-
> olulu if we are lucky). But I like the idea of a special issue. Can you tell me
> more about what are you thinking, what might be in the issue, what are some
> possible chapters, and why anyone would want to read it?

Reply by JA:

> Lots of questions—pass the mustard—and let me take a shot at a couple of
> them. We both know that concepts about needs and ways to assess them are
> constantly evolving. In the last six-to-seven years, at least nine books (and
> maybe more) about needs assessment have been written. You, I, and others
> have all published numerous articles, and the Needs Assessment TIG at AEA
> has taken on new life. So maybe the issue could capitalize on these events.
> One chapter, the first one, would have to capture what has been taking place
> and should be an overview of the field with a time line showing its origins
> and how it has progressed and changed (Altschuld & Watkins, Chapter 1 of
> this issue).

NEW DIRECTIONS FOR EVALUATION, no. 144, Winter 2014   © 2014 Wiley Periodicals, Inc., and the American Evaluation
Association.   Published online in Wiley Online Library (wileyonlinelibrary.com) • DOI: 10.1002/ev.20098

Response from RW about what might be missing:

I like it. And it would be great to have something about theory or at least theory-oriented. To me this is a shortcoming in much of what we see in practice and in academic writings. It just so happens that I have been discussing this notion with a colleague (Jolanta Kavale) in Lithuania who has interest in the philosophy of "needs" and perhaps we could work up a chapter about basic definitions of need—one that would sort of ask us to relook at the basics and subtle nature of what we mean by need (Watkins & Kavale, Chapter 2 of this issue).

Comment by JA:

I don't know, I was hoping to have higher standards in choosing authors.

To me, then, we would want a dose of real-world perceptions. From my point of view, needs assessments are prominent in some aspects of government work, in organizational development, and for identifying needs for training in the public and private sectors. A close personal friend and an evaluator of note, Molly Engle, has that first emphasis in her work, so why don't we invite her to write Chapter 3? If it is okay with her, I will join in for this chapter (Engle & Altschuld, Chapter 3 of this issue).

Going further, we know John Wedman's Performance Pyramid and its application really fits in with our thinking. He would be great for a chapter about organizations and private sector assessments. Let's ask him to write a chapter (Wedman, Chapter 4 of this issue). And then I am familiar with a unique training needs assessment that is currently underway in Ohio. (Go Bucks; you know I can't resist saying that at least once every time we talk.) But seriously, the project utilizes several different methods to collect data. I would suggest that Traci Lepicki and Adrienne Boggs, who are conducting that endeavor, could contribute a chapter (Lepicki & Boggs, Chapter 5 of this volume).

RW jumps in:

This is beginning to sound like lots of work. You will do all the heavy lifting, right?

Actually it will be fun to get to know some of these people better. Like you, I read their articles and occasionally see them present, but I don't know many of them all that well. And if we twist their arms a little maybe they will take over leading the TIG for us!

I think what we are talking about makes a lot of sense, but I perceive that we don't have anything of an international nature. Assessments are commonly

NEW DIRECTIONS FOR EVALUATION • DOI: 10.1002/ev

done in settings outside the U.S., and we don't want to paint ourselves as the middle of the needs assessment universe. As you know, I wrote a needs assessment book with friends at the World Bank; they have lots of international experience. Suppose we were to have a practical tips chapter for assessments outside the U.S., with examples coming from other countries. I could ask Maurya and another colleague at the Bank to take the lead on this (West Meiers, Watkins, & Marsh Song, Chapter 6 of this issue).

JA posits Chapter 7:

Along those lines, I have a new book (Sage Publishing) on the emergence of a hybrid model that combines asset/capacity building and needs assessment. I am working with Sonya and Yi-Fang to expand this concept and further develop this new approach. Suppose we build from this for a chapter. It would be cutting edge (Altschuld, Hung, & Lee, Chapter 7 of this issue).

RW comes back in:

I like the idea; let's go with it. Also, we have had many conversations about the future of needs assessment and issues that should be addressed. Should that be the final chapter, focusing on trends in practice and how technology will enhance what the future holds? Also, how can we improve what is being done and make assessments more rigorous? This would be a good closing note. What do you think (Watkins & Altschuld, Chapter 8 of this issue)?

JA has almost the final word:

I do have a concern, though. Although we have been talking about a great list of authors, I worry that we could get a kind of show-and-tell feel to the volume. Some of that is necessary and would ordinarily occur, but it cannot be the whole shooting match. Some of the audience for the issue may have more of an academic bent; how can we walk the tightrope between these competing types of things?

RW close to the final word:

Okay, what would you think about this? First, you do all work, then I take all the credit.

Just kidding! We have both edited books before so we can work together to strike a good balance. We also don't want it to be too academic; there is enough of that already out there. Second, let's guide them by asking challenging questions that take them a bit out of their comfort zone. What's your take?

JA eager to get the final word:

> I think it could work. But do you really have time for this? It is never easy to pull this many chapters together, and *New Directions* will be depending on us to deliver. Maybe we should chat with the authors we have mentioned, and then commit to a proposal once we know that we have enough people on-board.

> And since this is my idea, you are buying lunch!

James W. Altschuld
Ryan Watkins
Editors

JAMES W. ALTSCHULD is professor emeritus in the College of Education and Human Ecology, The Ohio State University.

RYAN WATKINS is an associate professor at George Washington University in Washington, DC, and founder of www.NeedsAssessment.org and www.WeShareScience.com.

NEW DIRECTIONS FOR EVALUATION • DOI: 10.1002/ev

Altschuld, J. W., & Watkins, R. (2014). A primer on needs assessment: More than 40 years
of research and practice. In J. W. Altschuld & R. Watkins (Eds.), *Needs assessment: Trends
and a view toward the future. New Directions for Evaluation, 144,* 5–18.

1

A Primer on Needs Assessment: More Than 40 Years of Research and Practice

James W. Altschuld, Ryan Watkins

Abstract

*This chapter consists of an overview of needs assessment's rich history, defi-
nitions, models, tools, and techniques. These closely align its theory, research,
and practice to several associated fields—most notably strategic planning and
evaluation. The highlights of the content include a comparison to—and differ-
entiation from—evaluation, a brief timeline of the recent history of the field, the
notable emergence of hybrid assessment and asset/capacity building approaches,
some discussion of opposition to needs assessment, and a description of two
prominent models that guide what assessors do. The summary captures the dynamic nature of the enterprise and how it is evolving.* © Wiley Periodicals,
Inc., and the American Evaluation Association.

Introduction

You may be asking what is a primer and why are the editors starting with
one? A primer is simply a book, or in this case a chapter, that is sometimes
used to get students started. Primers typically assume little prior knowledge
and focus on basic skills. For this *New Directions for Evaluation* issue, we are
taking some liberties with this description since most readers will have some
understanding of needs assessment. Yet, we believe that clarification and
amplification are desirable, since the topic can be complex and is frequently
misunderstood or misapplied.

NEW DIRECTIONS FOR EVALUATION, no. 144, Winter 2014 © 2014 Wiley Periodicals, Inc., and the American Evaluation
Association.   Published online in Wiley Online Library (wileyonlinelibrary.com) • DOI: 10.1002/ev.20099

In that light, the chapter explains what a needs assessment is and its relation to evaluation. From there is a brief historical discussion, followed by two prominent approaches to conducting an assessment. In conclusion, we offer a quick glimpse of several applications of basic needs assessment principles. Altogether, we hope that this primer will provide an adequate base from which you can gain the most from the chapters that follow.

Needs Assessment and Evaluation

A need in the simplest sense is a measurable gap between two conditions— what currently is and what should be. (Watkins & Kavale in Chapter 2 of this issue provide additional perspectives on defining needs.) This requires ascertaining what the circumstances are at a point in time, what is to be desired in the future, and a comparison of the two. Needs assessment also includes making judgments with regard to needs and putting them into prioritized order to guide decisions about what to do next.

Defining the gaps between what we want to accomplish and what we are currently achieving, and judging them in relation to one another, makes the endeavor rather complex (Rosen, 1991). The assessment process points to problem areas, issues, or difficulties that should be resolved. In most contexts, needs assessment focuses on gaps in results rather than in wants or possible solutions. Beyond that, tying needs assessments together with the identification of assets can provide valuable insights (see Altschuld, Hung, & Lee, Chapter 7 of this issue) and are best undertaken before beginning a new effort or before a decision about what to do has been made. Needs assessments are often considered a form of strategic or program planning even more than as a type of evaluation (see Wedman, Chapter 4 of this issue).

Usually when needs are assessed, several are found and there are limited resources for improvement (closure of those gaps), so, as mentioned previously, priorities must be set. Causal analysis, for example, may be employed to identify which gap might be most amenable to change and for which a solution strategy has a high likelihood of success (possibly based on evaluation from previous implementations). This is also helpful in thinking about how solutions could be done and when collecting evaluation data would be most useful. By identifying the desired/required state when determining needs, anticipated outcomes to measure later are brought into perspective. Further, it is to be noted that there are types of needs such as short- and long-term, maintenance, severe and slight, and others (Altschuld & Kumar, 2010).

Turning to evaluation, it may be thought of as the provision of information for making decisions about a program or project. Descriptions of evaluation frequently refer to formative and summative evaluation, though other frameworks can be applied (Fitzpatrick, Sanders, & Worthen, 2004). For formative evaluation, questions might be: Is the new entity taking place

NEW DIRECTIONS FOR EVALUATION • DOI: 10.1002/ev

as planned, is it performing well? How are the activities proceeding? What deviations are occurring? Are they on schedule? Are they working as intended? What snags are encountered, is the process being monitored, are appropriate data being collected, are in-course corrections being made, are the components of the program working in a complementary fashion, etc.? For summative, or bottom-line, impact, the questions concern: Has the project attained its objectives? Did it work in an equal fashion for all intended groups? Was it worth the expenditure of precious resources (time, personnel, materials, etc.)?

In contrast, needs assessment deals with questions such as What results should be accomplished at the societal, organizational, and individual levels? How do current results relate to desired results? How should we think about diverse needs in terms of importance? Which alternative solution strategies (or sets of solutions) can best reduce gaps in results? What criteria can be used to evaluate the alternatives?

Needs assessment is therefore at times more oriented to planning than evaluation, so you may be asking "Why is an issue of New Directions being devoted to it instead of one more firmly seated in evaluation?" In reality, the two concepts (and associated processes) are highly connected in methods and mission. This was very noticeable to a small national group of needs assessors who decided to affiliate with the American Evaluation Association (AEA) in the mid-1980s. What they observed was that the majority of programs and projects are predicated on quantified needs, perceived needs, or a combination of the two. If needs have been identified, prioritized, and their causes determined with solutions selected, these factors contribute directly to evaluation of the project or program—inevitably linking the two fields of study and practice.

In Table 1.1, evaluation and needs assessment are compared in relation to a number of key dimensions to demonstrate similar and unique properties. The table is intended to be illuminative, not comprehensive.

Other dimensions could be included in Table 1.1, but these hopefully suffice for clarifying why a national group of needs assessors selected AEA as its home. The two fields of study and practice are intertwined processes with a sharp demarcation between them being superficial, or even artificial. Needs assessment takes place early in the development of programs and feeds into the other, which is most common during implementation and operation. The idea of discrepancy readily applies when a program or project is being monitored or evaluated—thus the thinking is in tandem. Indeed, gaps in outcomes could be considered as input into recycling back to the need that guided the program's design in the first place.

One popular evaluation model (Context, Input, Process, and Product, or CIPP) developed by Stufflebeam in the 1960s (now being revisited by Stufflebeam & Coryn, 2014) embedded needs assessment into evaluation. More specifically, Context includes needs as the platform for new projects and interventions; from there, it moves to the examination of

Table 1.1. Evaluation and Needs Assessment: Some Similar and Unique Properties

Evaluation	Dimension	Needs Assessment
Evaluation occurs after a project or program has begun and often continuously thereafter.	Where does it take place in the life of a project or program?	Assessments occur before (or at the beginning) when an intervention, project, or program is implemented.
Determine how well the intervention is progressing and eventually achieves its intended ends.	Purpose of the activity	Determine important gaps and what ends are the targets, what are likely solution strategies, their key features, and what potentially might be evaluated in terms of anticipated results.
Logic maps, ideally developed during program planning, are used in evaluation as a guidepost for formative and summative evaluations.	Use of logic maps	Strategically define logic maps (or theories of change) to influence program or project design; causal analyses may lead to maps of solutions.
Evaluation practice calls for meaningful involvement of constituencies in identifying major outcomes and even in interpretation of obtained data.	Involvement of concerned constituencies	In the past, assessments were done more by the assessor, but following the lead of evaluation are now more inclusive of the active participation of constituencies (see Chapter 7 of this issue).
Evaluation utilizes a range of methods and views qualitative and quantitative ones as complementary.	Methods and procedures	In practice, they are similar to evaluation regarding a range of qualitative and quantitative methods, but there are several specialized to needs assessment due to the planning focus, including gap analysis, causal analysis, prioritization strategies, and procedures for comparing solution strategies.
Evaluation is incorporated into nearly every public endeavor as a requirement of granting agencies. It is part of the accountability scene.	Frequency of formal employment of the activity	Assessment is not observed as often as evaluation, perhaps because funding is often being linked to predetermined solutions and a desire to move quickly into action.

varied inputs (solutions) to deal with the inherent problems. For Stuffle-beam, assessment and evaluation could not be thought of apart from each other.

Other evaluation schema should be brought into the discussion. Empowerment and participatory approaches are strong in terms of the inclusion of involved groups and individuals in deciding what the evaluation is to be about—what variables are most critical to a project, how might they be measured, what should we be looking in terms of success, how would we know that a project is moving along properly, what levels of participation should be there, and so forth? Analogously, these are likewise characteristics of high-quality needs assessments and ones that are more frequently posited in the literature.

Assessments necessitate a careful examination of how to modify or even completely alleviate needs. They elucidate the best ways to do so and direct evaluators toward where to look at how programs operate and the impacts or effects they might have. This usually leads to greater program accountability and more sophisticated evaluations.

Opposition to Needs Assessment and the Emergence of Hybrids

As the concept of needs assessment was emerging in the 1960s and 1970s, sharp criticisms were appearing. One was that many of the then-new models were more heavily top-down, outside-in, and frequently those most affected by the needs came into the process as "subjects" instead of collaborators (or cotravelers) on the journey (Altschuld, 2014). Another concern was that most approaches were too focused on quantifying needs, pushing assessment to rely on indicators from databases or Likert-type scale surveys. Such assessments were not humanistic and did not get to the subtleties of the human condition that could be understood by utilizing qualitative data on perceived or felt needs for identifying deficiencies and opportunities. Because of these limitations, assessments were sometimes viewed as not very useful or a waste of time and money. Often they did not produce outcomes that led to significant, long-lasting change. Eventually, factors like these prompted the strident attack on the very premise of the enterprise.

In 1993, Kretzmann and McKnight noted that not much will come from assessing needs because they are seen as deficits, things that are wrong or amiss, or missing. This is fundamental to their argument (Altschuld, Hung, & Lee, Chapter 7 of this issue). When communities remain focused on deficits, they argued, they can lose direction and may not be empowered. The dependency mindset can constrain a community or organization, keeping it from seeing what is possible with the varied resources it has. In other words, the collective can become devoid of strength in their view. Seeking resources from outside is not necessarily a bad thing, but they assert it can rob the spirit and soul of power. Metaphorically, the argument is that the needs assessment process itself pushed people to see "the glass as half empty, not half full". Building from assets and capacities (half full) rather than solely needs (half empty) was viewed as a way to enhance moving ahead. For a time, this perspective led to an increasing number of asset/capacity building efforts rather than needs assessments in some public-sector contexts.

Of course, to continue the metaphor, the glass is both half full and half empty, so it is not that needs assessments at the time were giving an inaccurate view of the situation; rather, they were not giving the full picture. An approach that can strike a balance across both views is therefore potentially most useful. Recently, a hybrid of the two has been emerging, and many of such efforts include a healthy reverence for evaluation being part of them (Altschuld, 2014; Altschuld, Hung, & Lee, Chapter 7 of this issue). A comprehensive framework of needs assessment and asset/capacity building with evaluation integrated into it would be very utilitarian. Most of us today hopefully see these as intertwined processes within a system, not as separate or independent ones. It has taken some years to reach this point, with guidance from work both within the fields of needs assessment and evaluation, as well as from outside (e.g., systems theory, positive psychology, and appreciative inquiry). How has this transformation taken place? What were some of the main events and periods in the evolution of needs assessment to where it is today?

A Timeline for the Development of Needs Assessment

Going back to the very beginning of our existence as human beings we might suspect that need is embedded in our innate fiber. Coming very much forward from the murky start of us as a species, the Egyptian Book of the Dead contains references to what a person would "need" to survive in the afterlife. Of course, that assertion cannot be proved. Leap forward a few thousand years, and Hansen (1991) showed that we continued to attack problems and issues by looking at discrepancies (or needs), even if they were not called by that name. This was observed across fields and contexts. The idea of need for humans is also inherent in the writings of Abraham Maslow. But for this chapter, and the others in this issue, a distinction must be made that "need" refers to those of individuals and groups in organizational, community, and societal settings, not the Maslow connotation that focuses on psychological motivation.

Table 1.2 contains a number of historical events that have shaped understanding of needs and their assessment. Some significant contributors to the history of needs assessment, as well as evaluation, are also included. The table is a broad brushstroke, not a detailed listing of everything that has taken place and all contributors. It depicts, nevertheless, how NA progressed and evolved over time. The timeline starts in the mid-1960s when federal mandates with required needs assessments came onto the scene.

NEW DIRECTIONS FOR EVALUATION • DOI: 10.1002/ev

Table 1.2. Overview of Timeline of Modern Needs Assessment

Time Period	Nature of Event(s)	Contributors
The early years (mid-1950s to mid-1960s)	Maslow popularizes the concept of need in psychology and the term enters the national discourse on education	Bernard James questions the role of needs in defining educational goals (James, 1956) Congress of the United States
	Elementary and Secondary Education Act (ESEA) of 1965 called for the determination of the needs for programs and projects	Stufflebeam develops early version of CIPP
	CIPP evaluation model produced in 1965	
The formative period (mid-1960s through about 1980)	Many needs assessments being done, especially in public schools	Tom Gilbert begins the dialogue of needs in terms of training requirements (Gilbert, 1967)
	Major study of those assessments	Witkin conducts nationwide study of needs assessments conducted in school districts
	Writings and presentations of some prominent authors	Warheit et al. book is written (Warheit, Bell, & Schwab, 1977)
	Prominent criticisms appear	Kaufman begins development of his Organizational Elements Model and publishes several books (see Notes below) on conducting needs assessment (especially with the education sector)
		Scriven and Roth paper published in *New Directions for Program Evaluation* (Scriven & Roth, 1978)
		Kamis' major analysis of the criticisms of NA; Monette's critique of philosophical assumptions (Kamis, 1979)
		The first (and only) National Needs Assessment Conference was held in Oakland, California. The conference was sponsored by the National Institute of Education and the International Society of Educational Planners

(Continued)

Table 1.2. Continued

Time Period	Nature of Event(s)	Contributors
Coming of age but some headwinds (1980s through the early 1990s)	A heyday of watershed events in NA	Witkin, Kaufman, Neuber, and Lauffer all produce books on various aspects of the topic (see Notes below)
	At least four major books are written and gain wide acceptance	
	Small number of courses devoted to NA are at several universities	Courses on needs assessment within evaluation programs get started at Southern Illinois, Utah State, and Ohio State; already integrated in instructional curricula in several programs
	Small national needs assessment group joins AEA	Rossett popularized term in the training field (Rossett, 1987)
	Criticisms reappear toward the latter part of the period	The models or approaches of Witkin and Kaufman take shape
Productive years but challenges (Early 1990s through the early 2000s)	Rejoinders to the criticisms by Witkin	Witkin takes on the critics
	Attack on needs assessment from an asset/capacity building stance	Kretzmann and McKnight harshly note the negatives of assessment (Kretzmann & McKnight, 1993)
	Asset/capacity building efforts take off based on wanting to start from a positive not needs-oriented position	Altschuld and Witkin write two books and Gupta generates one oriented toward business settings (Altschuld & Witkin, 2000; Gupta, 1999)
	Major new books on NA are published	Kaufman continues to publish several books on needs assessments (especially within private-sector organizations)
		Scriven and Roth paper reissued by the American Evaluation Association

(Continued)

Table 1.2. Continued

Time Period	Nature of Event(s)	Contributors
Building a foundation for things to come (Early 2000s through nearly the end of the decade)	Major paper about the placement of NA in organizations Papers about the Performance Pyramid and the NA and evaluation survey Persistence of NA-TIG group at AEA as a viable entity Emergence of hybrid-like needs assessment and asset/capacity building efforts appear More books about needs assessment	For papers see Altschuld, Wedman, and Watkins, and Watkins and Kaufman, each pushing needs assessment in new directions The five-volume Needs Assessment Kit, edited by Altschuld (see Notes below) Gupta, Sleezer, and Russ-Eft (2014)
Coming into fruition and maturity (2010 to the present)	Books continuing to appear, applications in international situations More examples of hybrid assessment are seen in the literature This issue is produced	Gupta, Sleezer, and Russ-Eft; Watkins, West Meiers, and Visser; Kaufman and Guerra; and Altschuld all produce new books on needs assessments

Notes: An animated timeline is available at www.NeedsAssessment.org. The co-authors also suggest that readers consult the following supplemental sources which are in chronological order: James (1956); Gilbert (1967); Stufflebeam (1968); Kaufman (1972); English and Kaufman (1975); Kamis (1979); Warheit et al. (1977); Scriven and Roth (1978); Monette (1979); Kaufman and English (1979); Neuber, Atkins, Jacobson, and Reuterman (1980); Lauffer (1982); Rossett (1987); Kaufman (1992); Kaufman (1998); Gupta (1999); Kaufman (2000); Watkins and Kaufman (2002); Altschuld (2004); Gupta, Sleezer, and Russ-Eft (2007); Altschuld (2010); Watkins, West Meiers, and Visser (2012); and Gupta, Sleezer, and Russ-Eft (2014).

Parsing all the history and exceptional contributions that have shaped the study and practice of needs assessment is beyond the scope of the primer. In our judgment, however, two seminal contributions are most salient to understanding how needs assessment has evolved in recent decades, and those are the models (or approaches) of Belle Ruth Witkin and Roger Kaufman. We should mention that the coeditors have been influenced deeply by, and have been long-term collaborators with, both these thought leaders in the field. Kaufman and Witkin were pioneers, and indeed friends. Through their mentorship both also planted the strong roots that sustained the field as it grew. Witkin died in 1998, while Kaufman continues to be an active contributor (Kaufman & Guerra-Lopez, 2013).

The Approaches of Witkin and Kaufman

In 1984, Witkin published what has come to be seen as the theoretical tome on the topic. In that book she mentioned, although not prominently, a three-phase model of assessment that was in its early stages of development. By the early 1990s, she along with the first coeditor (Altschuld) were ready to push the field forward with a new book and systematized approach to needs assessment (Witkin & Altschuld, 1995). In it, they greatly expanded explanations of the three phases, including the steps and tools within each. Later, the analysis of what might be done in each phase continued to expand (Altschuld & Kumar, 2010; Altschuld & Witkin, 2000). Based on Witkin's original conceptualization, the most recent version of the three-phase approach is provided in Table 1.3.

Concurrent to the advancements being offered by Witkin (and subsequently by Witkin and Altschuld), Kaufman was applying a systems-engineering perspective to the goals of identifying and prioritizing needs. Initially focusing on U.S. educational reform in the 1970s and later on finding applications in both global public and private institutions, applying the systems perspective to needs assessment led to Kaufman's Organization Elements Model (OEM) as a key element of systemic assessment and planning. Not to be confused with a process model (such as the three-phase approach described above), the OEM is a framework with three eternally linked types of needs: gaps in results at the societal level (Mega), organizational level (Macro), and individual/team level (Micro). Discrepancies at each of these levels of the framework then must be aligned with the Processes and Inputs that drive the system (Table 1.4). Kaufman's influential writings on the OEM, and the processes for assessing needs within his framework, largely provided a specialized theory base for needs assessments.

Summary

This primer on needs assessment is intended to provide an overview of the field's rich history, definitions, models, tools, and techniques that closely

Table 1.3. Witkin's Three Phases of Needs Assessment (as Updated in Altschuld & Kumar, 2010)

Phase	Nature	Methods' Overview
Phase 1: Preassessment	The purpose is to do reconnaissance to see what the situation is about: Is there a need or are there needs, and are they of sufficient scope and depth to be pursued further (usually under the aegis of an organization or community Needs Assessment Committee [NAC])? The phase relies on existing information and data before going into the expensive and time-consuming second one. Phase 1 could lead to decisions such as do nothing more because the needs aren't there; go to Phase 2 and do more extensive data collection; or go to Phase 3 (action plans to resolve the needs uncovered).	Data in records Databases Information from the literature Data existing of routinely kept by external agencies Evaluation reports if available Informal or a small set of interviews Observations Other methods as appropriate
Phase 2: Assessment	If Phase 1 did not provide enough understanding about needs and more was required, you enter into Phase 2. In-depth surveying, deeper analyses of existing sources, looking for more information, detailed exploration of the literature, and intensifying the collection of data. This phase may get into such things as the causal analysis of needs (possibly to looking for potential solution strategies) and the prioritization of needs. Decisions are to go no further or that we know enough and have needs-based priorities to plan and initiate solutions (Phase 3).	Formal and specialized surveying Individual and focus group interviews Collecting more literature to illuminate needs and solutions Formal causal analyses Formal prioritization strategies Other procedures as appropriate
Phase 3: Postassessment	Taking what was learned in Phases 1 and 2 and beginning to initiate actions to rectify needs. Phase 3 overlaps with the last part of Phase 2, so, if necessary, some of the activities might be done in more detail. Hopefully, in this phase we might get to implementing action plans and evaluating how well the solutions were working. Lastly, this phase would include strategies for evaluating the needs assessment itself.	Many of the procedures indicated above, especially formal and in-depth causal analyses and prioritization Action plan related activities such as benchmarking, multiattribute utility theory Formative and summative evaluation procedures

Table 1.4. Kaufman's OEM (as Updated in Kaufman & Guerra-Lopez, 2013)

Organizational Element	Examples	Needs Assessment Level	Type of Planning	Key Stakeholder
Outcomes: societal results and consequences	Quality of life, health, self-sufficiency; gainfully employed graduates	Mega	Strategic planning	Clients, client's clients, community, society
Outputs: organizational results	Profits, sales, patients discharged, graduates	Macro	Tactical planning	Organization itself
Products: en-route results or building blocks; note there may be multiple levels of products	Competent employees, courses completed, assembled vehicles, medical procedures completed, accomplished/met standards	Micro	Operational Planning	Individual and groups of employees or performers
Processes: interventions, solutions, methods	Teaching, training, learning, manufacturing, selling, managing, marketing	Quasi	Action planning	Individual and groups of employees or performers
Inputs: resources	Funding, employees, equipment, regulations, standards	Quasi	Resource planning	Individual and groups of employees or performers

align its theory, research, and practice. At the same time, we have hopefully illustrated that needs assessment is closely associated with, and works in conjunction with, several other fields—most notably strategic planning and evaluation, sometimes borrowing on the tools and techniques of both to guide practice and at other times deriving theoretical constructs to shape research. As a result, we believe, needs assessment has undergone several transformations over the past half century to become a dynamic field that improves the quality of decisions being made in a wide variety of contexts.

The history of needs assessment is likewise rich on several dimensions, including that it (a) is largely influenced by public- and private-sector applications (see Engle & Altschuld, Chapter 3 of this issue; Wedman, Chapter 4 of this issue; and Lepicki & Boggs, Chapter 5 of this issue); (b) draws extensively on the literature of varied disciplines, including but not limited to evaluation; and (c) has continued to evolve while other related processes became yesterday's fad. Though much smaller in scale than other sister fields (e.g., evaluation), needs assessment has been able to maintain its utility to practitioners while developing its own research-based theoretical foundations and specialized tools. Fueled by exceptionally productive thought leaders, such as Witkin and Kaufman, the field has continued to flourish within varied contexts (evaluation, performance improvement, and organizational development). In its latest stage, the future of needs assessment as it moves to integrate asset/capacity building looks bright.

References

Altschuld, J. W. (2004). Emerging dimensions of needs assessment. *Performance Improvement, 43*(1), 10–15.

Altschuld, J. W. (Ed.). (2010). *The needs assessment kit.* Thousand Oaks, CA: Sage.

Altschuld, J. W. (2014). *Bridging the gap between asset/capacity building and needs assessment: Concepts and practical applications.* Thousand Oaks, CA: Sage.

Altschuld, J. W., & Kumar, D. D. (2010). *Needs assessment: An overview.* Thousand Oaks, CA: Sage.

Altschuld, J. W., & Witkin, B. R. (2000). *From needs assessment to action: Translating needs into solution strategies.* Thousand Oaks, CA: Sage.

English, F. W., & Kaufman, R. (1975). *Needs assessment: Focus for curriculum development.* Washington, DC: Association for Supervision and Curriculum Development (ASCD).

Fitzpatrick, J. L., Sanders, J. R., & Worthen, B. R. (2004). *Program evaluation: Alternative approaches and practical guidelines.* Boston, MA: Pearson Education.

Gilbert, T. (1967). Praxeonomy: A systematic approach to identifying training needs. *Management of Personnel Quarterly, 6*(3), 20–33.

Gupta, K. (1999). *A practical guide to needs assessment.* San Francisco, CA: Pfeiffer.

Gupta, K., Sleezer, C. M., & Russ-Eft, D. F. (2007). *A practical guide to needs assessment.* San Francisco, CA: Pfeiffer.

Gupta, K., Sleezer, C. M., & Russ-Eft, D. F. (2014). *A practical guide to needs assessment.* San Francisco, CA: Pfeiffer.

Hansen, D. J. (1991). *An empirical study of the structure of needs assessment* (Unpublished doctoral dissertation). The Ohio State University, Columbus.

James, B. (1956). Can 'Needs' define educational goals? *Adult Education*, 6, 95–100.

Kamis, E. (1979). A witness for the defense of needs assessment. *Evaluation and Program Planning*, 2(1), 7–12.

Kaufman, R. (1972). *Educational system planning*. Englewood Cliffs, NJ: Prentice Hall.

Kaufman, R. (1992). *Strategic planning plus*. Thousand Oaks, CA: Sage.

Kaufman, R. (1998). *Strategic thinking: A guide to identifying and solving problems* (Revised ed.). Washington, DC: The International Society for Performance Improvement and the American Society for Training and Development.

Kaufman, R. (2000). *Mega planning: Practical tools for organizational success*. Thousand Oaks, CA: Sage.

Kaufman, R., & English, F. W. (1979). *Needs assessment: Concept and application*. Englewood Cliffs, NJ: Educational Technology Publications.

Kaufman, R., & Guerra-Lopez, I. (2013). *Needs assessment for organizational success*. Alexandria, VA: ASTD Press.

Kretzmann, J. P., & McKnight, J. L. (1993). *Building communities from the inside out*. Chicago, IL: ACTA Publications.

Lauffer, A. (1982). *Assessment tools: For practitioners, managers, and trainers*. Beverly Hills, CA: Sage.

Monette, M. L. (1979). Need assessment: A critique of philosophical assumptions. *Adult Education Quarterly*, 29(2), 83–95.

Neuber, K. A., Atkins, W. T., Jacobson, J. A., & Reuterman, N. A. (1980). *Needs assessment: A model for community planning*. Beverly Hills, CA: Sage.

Rosen, R. (1991). *Life itself: A comprehensive inquiry into the nature, origin, and fabrication of life*. New York, NY: Columbia University Press.

Rossett, A. (1987). *Training needs assessment*. Englewood Cliffs, NJ: Educational Technology Publishing.

Scriven, M., & Roth, J. (1978). Needs assessment: Concept and practice. *New Directions for Program Evaluation*, 1978, 1–11. doi:10.1002/ev.1196

Stufflebeam, D. L. (1968). *Evaluation as enlightenment for decision-making*. Columbus: Ohio State University Evaluation Center.

Stufflebeam, D. L., & Coryn, C. L. S. (2014). *Evaluation theory, models, and applications* (2nd ed.). New York: Wiley.

Warheit, G., Bell, R. A., & Schwab, J. (1977). *Needs assessment approaches: Concepts and methods* (Dept. of Health, Education, and Welfare Publication No. (ADM) 77-472). Washington, DC: Superintendent of Documents, U.S. Government Printing Office.

Watkins, R., & Kaufman, R. (2002). Assessing and evaluating: Differentiating perspectives. *Performance Improvement Journal*, 41(2), 22–28.

Watkins, R., West Meiers, M., & Visser, Y. I. (2012). *A guide to assessing needs*. Washington, DC: International Bank for Reconstruction and Development/International Development Association or the World Bank.

Witkin, B. R. (1984). *Assessing needs in educational and social programs: Using information to make decisions, set priorities, and allocate resources*. San Francisco, CA: Jossey-Bass.

Witkin, B. R., & Altschuld, J. W. (1995). *Planning and conducting needs assessments: A practical guide*. Thousand Oaks, CA: Sage.

JAMES W. ALTSCHULD is professor emeritus in the College of Education and Human Ecology, The Ohio State University.

RYAN WATKINS is an associate professor at George Washington University in Washington, DC, and founder of www.NeedsAssessment.org and www.WeShareScience.com.

Watkins, R., & Kavale, J. (2014). Needs: Defining what you are assessing. In J. W. Altschuld & R. Watkins (Eds.), *Needs assessment: Trends and a view toward the future. New Directions for Evaluation, 144,* 19–31.

2

Needs: Defining What You Are Assessing

Ryan Watkins, Jolanta Kavale

Abstract

By definition your needs assessment should assess needs, but how do you define them? Further, how do you operationalize that definition to measure needs? Do your partners and stakeholders also hold the same conceptual, and operational, definitions? Is there agreement that the project is only going to assess needs and not wants, assets, capacity, or solutions? Or are you really expected to assess all five? Each of these is an important consideration that can substantially influence the success of any needs assessment. In this chapter, the authors examine how definitions and use of the word need influence the design and implementation of an assessment, suggesting that the definition can shape the results of what is found. © Wiley Periodicals, Inc., and the American Evaluation Association.

Introduction

What is a "need"? On the surface it sounds like an easy question. Yet this word, which is fundamental to all needs assessments, has not gotten much attention of late. In the 1960s and 1970s, there was a vibrant conversation on what constitutes needs and needs assessments (Bradshaw, 1972; Monette, 1979; Witkin, 1984), but the debate in the literature has not continued in recent years—even though agreement on a definition remains elusive. Today, numerous ones are used, and many times in research and practice no precise definition is applied at all.

From needs being seen exclusively as gaps in results to needs incorporating values, wants, and assets, the definition delineates the scope of your assessment. More specifically, how you define needs (a) clarifies the goals of your assessment; (b) influences how you design your assessment; (c) determines what you measure, and therefore how you measure; and (d) influences what you report, to whom, and in what format. In this chapter, we review how theorists and practitioners define needs across varied disciplines, how these definitions may influence your next needs assessment, and what potential challenges a definition (or a lack thereof) can create for implementing a successful assessment.

Why Needs Are Important in Evaluation Practice

The effectiveness of a program or project is often measured by evaluating responsiveness to the needs of participants, organizations, donors, communities, or others. As a consequence, many "participatory approaches" of evaluation, for example, place a particular emphasis on the needs of clients (Brandt, 2011; Meyer, 2011; Stockman, 2011). The clear definition and measurement of needs, for one or more of these stakeholder groups, is therefore considered an essential component in most evaluation practices. Further, this focus on needs separates evaluation practice from other complementary approaches of quality assurance (auditing, lean six sigma, etc.).

As a result, on a daily basis, professionals, consultants, counselors, evaluators, and others are approached with statements and questions that relate to needs, such as "We need an evaluation of our program," "Which groups' needs should we address first?" or "They really need to get their act together; can you help?" People and organizations after all have a common requirement to know how they are doing at meeting needs—their own or those of others—in order to make decisions about what to do next.

In practice, needs are also disguised in common expressions—for example, when someone says "we have a problem," "that team's results are unsatisfactory," or "our return-on-investment is negative." These typically indicate that there is an undefined need. This is true to the extent that often clients seeking an evaluation are not aware of the professional use of the term "need" or "needs assessment." Thus, it becomes the task of the assessor (or evaluator) to uncover and think about the hidden meanings in such cases.

Yet no matter how they are described, needs exist in all organizations, communities, and societies. And the act of labeling them as needs (even if other expressions are used) suggests their existence and requires some action. Such knowledge helps evaluators to determine the effectiveness of the program and frequently forms the basis for future actions (or inactions). Likewise, in needs assessment practice the identification and prioritization of needs is the primary goal of the activity (Kaufman & Guerra-Lopez, 2013).

Without a clear definition of need, it is difficult (if not impossible) to objectively evaluate results, determine quality, and make justifiable

NEW DIRECTIONS FOR EVALUATION • DOI: 10.1002/ev

decisions about what to do next. For example, community leaders must frequently weigh the "need" of one group for public transportation against that of another group for lower cost utilities. Or in an organization, they ask how the "need" of health benefits for employees is related to those of clients for lower cost products. When people talk of their needs or those of others, they most often think of tangible results, values, wants, existing assets, and/or preferred solutions —making comparisons of needs often misleading and making effective decision making a challenge (Nutt, 2008). Without a consistent and agreed upon meaning, decisions have to be made based on unequal comparisons (apples to oranges).

Searching for Meaning

Satisfying of needs may be a motivator of our actions, but in modern use, the word "need" appears to have lost a clear sense of meaning. This is not unexpected. Bremner (1956) suggested that the concept of human need tends to be periodically rediscovered, and we contend that it is appropriate to reinvigorate the conversation once again in order to guide needs assessment research and practice.

Needs are often defined and interpreted differently when applying the conceptual systems of various disciplines or examining them across contexts, ranging from government policy making to organizational management to community development. Wright, Williams, and Wilkinson (1998) noted that doctors, sociologists, philosophers, and economists all have unique views of what needs are (and are not). Likewise, psychologists and educators use other frameworks to define needs. This lack of a unifying perspective (Doyal & Gough, 1991) is troubling, leaving researchers and practitioners working in such areas to search for their own meaning.

This is not new, of course. Since Aristotle, people have struggled with need, and by the 1970s the issue was at the forefront in the emergence of needs assessment as a field of practice. Witkin (1984) provides a useful discussion of definitions and frameworks that engaged the needs assessment and evaluation communities during this period. But in the decades that followed, the debate has not continued.

Experience alone does not create knowledge. (Kurt Lewin, 1946)

As exceptions, current philosophy literature does debate on definitions of needs (e.g., Wiggins, 2005), as does the literature on "human needs" (especially in international development). There the focus is on how to define needs, in the light of increasing awareness of limited societal resources for satisfying them. Yet, there is still no clear distinction between objective needs (childhood mortality rates, etc.) and subjective needs (expanding democracy, etc.). But this has not led to a consensus definition within these fields, nor one that can be practically applied across diverse areas and professional practices (including needs assessment and evaluation).

Further, there is not even agreement on whether "need" is a positive or negative term (Table 2.1). In the positive, "needs" are often used as placeholders as goods, nutriments, positive environment, commodities, or things (as in "basic necessities") to be provided and secured. In other cases, "need" carries an undesirable connotation, meaning deprivation, deficiency, lack, harm, discrepancy, or gap that has to be identified and avoided. Lastly, needs can be associated with drives, goals, and potential that cannot be directly linked to a positive or negative category of meaning, as seen most clearly in the psychology literature (Maslow's hierarchy of needs as motivators).

Without clear and accepted guidance, through our choice of words we routinely (and often carelessly) apply the label of need to objects or goods (a house, a latte), to activities (exercise, paying taxes), and even to psychological states (self-actualization), leading you to hear comments like "I need to a new car" or "they need to take training." By doing so, we quickly elevate the perceived importance of these objects, activities, or states from things we desire to things that we can't live without, even when we would not consciously argue for such a high level of perceived importance.

Further, without a definition, the relative importance cannot readily be measured or questioned, nor can alternatives for meeting the needs be effectively weighed. For example, how can an organization trying to reduce costs choose between reducing healthcare benefits and reducing vacation days without a clear specification of employee needs? Employees commonly refer to each (healthcare benefits and vacation days) as "needs," though the two are obviously not equivalent on all dimensions.

Qualifying needs with terms such as "relevant," "special," "basic," "essential," "universal," "absolute," or "vital" without offering ways to distinguish them can also increase the motivational power of the word. Who can argue against providing resources for meeting the "basic" or "universal" needs of people? Indeed, the motivational power inherent in labeling something as a need (or a "vital" or an "absolute" one) could lead to abuse of the term—making it all the more important that needs assessments and evaluations, as well as other activities contingent on needs, work from an agreed upon meaning of the word.

Another concern in the search for a shared meaning is the politics often associated with whose expertise decides what is a need (Lister, 2010). Clarke and Langan (1998, p. 260) stated that the "question of how the needs of different individuals, or groups of individuals, are met in our society is not so straightforward. It is immediately apparent that there is considerable conflict over the ways in which society defines and meets the needs of particular individuals or sections of society." This challenge has led some professionals to avoid the concept of need all together, including some philosophers (Reader, 2005) and economists (McCain, 2011); this has also been found in social work, education, and several other social

Table 2.1. Common Categories of Meanings of the Term "Need"

Object-Focused Definitions

A thing	Denotes *a thing* without which it is impossible to live, such as one cannot live without breathing or nourishment (Wiggins, 1987).
Things	*Things* without which someone will be seriously harmed or else will live a life that is vitally impaired (Wiggins, 2005).
Commodities	The *commodities* that are indispensably necessary to support life, and whatever custom renders indecent or intolerable for anyone to be without (Smith, 1776).

Goals

Sets of goals, drives	*Sets of goals* (also called basic needs or drives): physiological, safety, love, esteem, and self-actualization (Maslow, 1943, 1970a, 1970b).
Category of goals	"Need refers to a particular *category of goals* which are believed to be universalisable" (Gough, 2002, p. 7).
Environment	An *environment* in which an animate creature won't flourish unless it has it (Anscombe, 1958/1981).

Deficiencies

Objective deficiencies	*Objective deficiencies* that actually exist and may or may not be recognized by the person who has the need (Atwood & Ellis, 1971).
Deprivations and potential	Finite, few, and classifiable, needs are both as *deprivations and potential* (Max-Neef, Elizalde, & Hopenhayn, 1991).

Gaps

Gap in results	Gap in results *between "what is" and "what should be"* (Kaufman, 1996).
Gap in conditions	A learning or performance *gap* between the current condition and the desired condition (Gupta, Sleezer, & Russ-Eft, 2007).
Discrepancy of states	Measured *discrepancy* between the current state and the desired one (Altschuld & Lepicki, 2010).
What we require	"Our human needs are *what we require* to function minimally well as the kinds of creatures we are" (Brock, 2005, p. 65).

Human Condition

Necessary conditions and aspirations	The *necessary conditions and aspirations* of full human functioning (Hamilton, 2006).
Means, ends, drives, and goals	Human needs take the form of *means or ends* and *drives or goals* depending on context; together, they constitute different equally significant moments in human existence and human individuality and freedom and are therefore not solely means but means and ends (Hamilton, 2003).
Energy or information required or lacking	"A need is *matter-energy or information* that is useful or *required* but potentially *lacking* in some degree according to a purpose of a living system" (Tracy, 1983, p. 598).

Physical/Psychological

Nutriments	" . . . *nutriments* that must be procured by a living entity to maintain its growth, integrity, and health (whether physiological or psychological)" (Ryan & Deci, 2000, p. 326).
A lack of objective requirement	"An *objective requirement* to avoid a state of illness" (Mallmann & Marcus, 1980, p. 165).

science disciplines. This, however, does not resolve the underlying issue of need (see, McCain, 2011) and it is not a practical option for those conducting needs assessments.

Conceptualizing Needs

Conceptualizing needs, as a precursor to starting a needs assessment, points to several key relationships that should shape your definition.

Needs Versus Solutions

Even well-intending authors and practitioners in many disciplines get tangled in the distinction between needs and solutions to needs. Routinely, they do not get past the solution (sun as solution for growing a plant, or training as a solution to employee performance problems) as the definition of the need. Other examples at the individual level include employment and self-actualization, whereas at the organizational level there are growth and profit. This entanglement leads to the focus on solutions to needs rather than a pragmatic definition of what needs are that can be applied across contexts which would permit objective examinations of alternative solutions for achieving the same results (see the open systems principle of equifinality; von Bertalanffy, 1969).

Noun Versus Verb

From "you need to buy this car" to "they need Internet access," when need is used as a verb it takes us into looking at solutions before we know what results are to be achieved by those solutions. This is so prevalent in today's lexicon that is hard to escape—such as when a child says "I need that toy." Greenwald (1975) noted that when people use need as a verb ("I need a new car"), they cut their options to one and don't realize that other options are possible (a bike, bus, or train) to achieve the same results. By using need as a noun ("my need is to get to work in less time"), you have a basis for comparing potential solutions and guiding decisions—two key tasks of an effective needs assessment.

Needs Versus Wants

On the surface, most people will readily agree that needs are not the same as wants. But without providing guidance it is easy to confuse the two, with really strong wants (or desires) often being elevated to the status of needs.

The distinction is especially important when conducting a needs assessment. Assessing wants can help us determine what people desire, but doing so rarely reflects their actual needs (via a consistent definition of the term). As Hamilton (2006) points out, "Needs are not simply strong wants" (p. 228). Further, "wanting something does not entail needing it, and vice versa, someone may have a need without having a desire for what he needs and, he may have a desire without having a need for what he wants" (Frankfurt, 1998, p. 30).

Yet, needs and wants are often closely associated. McLeod (2011) suggests that "needs themselves are not to be confused with the desires they generate" (p. 215). In other words, in needs assessment you must ensure that needs (increased productivity or reduction in gender-based violence) are not confused with desired solutions (such as more training for staff or gender-segregated schools). These might end up as recommended solutions in some contexts, but they are not needs. Thus, a prerequisite step to distinguishing needs and wants is to define what you mean by needs in your assessment.

Absolute Versus Relative Needs

McLeod (2011) distinguishes between absolute and relative needs. McLeod (2011) and others (including Wiggins) define absolute needs as " ... involve[ing] both necessity and dependency" (p. 212), such as a flower "needs" sunlight to grow. Science, of course, continually challenges our conceptions of absolute needs, including the requirement of sunlight for growing plants. What may be absolute needs today may not be so tomorrow, and very few professional contexts (outside of, potentially, the physiological and biological sciences) have much application for absolutism.

This leaves the focus on relative (or normative) needs as the more pragmatic basis for defining needs. In other words, most needs assessments are done within the context of the society, the organization, and the perceptions of the people at that point in time. This is not to assert that normative needs are not important; they are, yet it must be recognized that needs typically shift over time (including that some needs are met, new ones emerge, and technologies change how we address needs).

Individual Versus Group Versus Societal Needs

There is often a popular assumption that needs are the premises of individuals. Maslow's *Hierarchy of Needs* in psychology focuses solely on individual-level needs. Nevertheless, groups (such as organizations and institutions) also have needs (increased client satisfaction, productivity that meets consumer demand). Societies have needs (reductions in greenhouse gases or decreases in gender-based violence).

According to Reader (2005), for Plato and Aristotle, needs are as much properties of individuals as they are of states. Aristotle suggested that "the same life is best for each individual, and for states and for mankind collectively" (1325b31; bl4–32). At Politics VII §8 Aristotle further discusses the necessities of the state. For Aristotle, the state first arises out of human necessities (Reader, 2005).

Kaufman (2011), in his definition of need, further emphasized that needs be assessed at the society, organization, and individual levels. Needs, and therefore definitions of what needs are, exist within multiple contexts ranging from a single person (a staff member's number of sales) to an organization (a business' number of defective products being delivered to clients) to our shared society (new cases of tuberculosis).

Need Versus Type of Need

To differentiate needs, qualifiers are often added to the term to indicate a particular type of need (basic needs, training needs, client needs, patients' needs, etc.), and as a result a variety of needs assessments are created: training needs assessment, client needs assessment, and so forth. These may seem to be practical terms for describing the focus of your needs assessment (or evaluation), but they do not define what the need is (or is not) on their own, and they often confuse the focus of the assessment. By calling it a "training needs assessment," you are inferring (and communicating to others) that training is the solution for whatever needs you identify and that those not associated with training solutions will be ignored. This erodes objectivity and leads to an assessment that is often little more than a solution in search of a problem (Triner, Greenberry, & Watkins, 1996).

While there are other relationships that we can reflect on when designing, developing, and implementing a needs assessment, those mentioned earlier are some of the essentials. Each points to why defining needs is critical for guiding professional practice.

Influence of a Definition

Defining needs may seem like an academic exercise or a theoretical debate with little impact or value for practice. This could not be further from the truth. Defining what you are assessing is the foundation to a successful assessment, with implications to multiple aspects of the associated tasks.

Designing Your Assessment

In the end, a needs assessment should help inform decisions about what to do next (Rossett, 1989, 1995). Thus, when designing an assessment, you should first focus the design on the decisions that will have to be made (or questions to be answered) using the results. This type of backward design process, borrowed from numerous disciplines, will guide the design and ensure that the assessment achieves valuable results.

Decisions about what to do next typically hinge on the ability of people to define the results they want to accomplish. The challenges of this are often overlooked, and assessments frequently focus too early on measuring the current state based on the assumption that people agree on the measurable goals and objectives for the future. In most cases, needs do come with either an explicit or implicit expectation that there is a desired condition—the explicit expectation that "all reports going to clients will meet all five quality standards," or the implicit expectation that "we must improve the quality of reports before they go to clients." Such expectations affect the design of a needs assessment.

Explicit expectations of results can usually be applied in the determination of needs very easily. For example, if "currently 30% of reports meet all five quality standards," then the need would represent the other 70%. On the other hand, when desired results are not explicitly defined (or assumed and not discussed), it is essential that needs assessment provide the context for clarifying the desired results.

Continuing the example, if it is only agreed that the quality of reports should be improved (or some other vague statement of intent), then it is difficult (if not impossible) to systematically determine what to do next. As Lewis Carroll (1865) reminded us in *Alice in Wonderland*, if you don't know where you are going, any road will get you there. Therefore, by measuring needs, evaluators and other professionals also must deal with measuring and validating the goals (desired results) that create, or at least help define, the need.

Unfortunately, many needs assessments are not designed with either a focus on future results to be achieved or the current results being accomplished. When needs are defined by solutions (training, new software, more schools), they really identify or justify times when the previously selected solution can be applied. A solution-focused assessment may try to answer what training has to offer by relying on interviews with managers who have responsibilities for it within an organization or on a survey of staff asking them what training they want to take in the next year. In both instances, this could be a self-fulfilling prophecy; if you ask people what training they want to offer or take, then they will tell you what training they want regardless of its link to future results.

Conversely, doing assessments properly can help guide decisions about what to do next. And professionals conducting them require appropriate tools to not only assess the need but also to define (or clarify) the long-term vision, mission, and goals behind it.

Implementing Your Assessment

During implementation of an assessment, how you define needs impacts the data collected and the techniques used to obtain the information. If you are using the needs as gaps in results definition, then methods, instruments, and data analysis all include a strong focus on the two results (desired vs. current) that define gaps. Your survey contains questions on what are the desired results of activities and what current results are being achieved.

NEW DIRECTIONS FOR EVALUATION • DOI: 10.1002/ev

Similarly, your interviews explore how success is defined and how progress in that direction is being monitored.

Whereas if needs are studied from an object-focused definition (Table 2.1), then the data you collect and the tools used will be different. You may ask about the things people perceive as necessary to avoid harm (water, transportation, cell phones, etc.) and ask questions about the barriers they face when acquiring what they "need." Here you may choose a simple survey to measure these desires, while focus groups may be used to consider the relationships among perceived needs.

Who participates in your assessment may also vary depending on the definition of need being applied. After all, those who know what results should be, and are being achieved (such as a production line manager who implements lean six sigma or total quality management), are valuable participants in an assessment focused on results. Alternatively, for a physical/psychological definition of need (see Table 2.1), providers of medical and psychological treatment would be key participants.

How data are analyzed is also shaped by the definition. With a gaps definition, for example, you examine the size of the gaps, where they are located, the direction of the gaps, and demographics associated with them (Watkins, West Meiers, & Visser, 2012). A small-sized gap, as an illustration, in the performance of sales people in documenting leads, may be a higher priority than a medium-sized one in following up with clients after sales.

In comparison, with an object-focused definition (Table 2.1) you might look more on differences in preferences across demographic groups. Here, the data might indicate that a large percentage of sales staff believe that tablet computers would be beneficial for documenting leads, whereas sales managers may perceive that financial incentives are required.

These and other implementation differences may seem subtle in many cases where the definition will have significant implications for budgets, personnel requirements, timeframes, and other considerations in the assessment process. Hence it is important to be clear and consistent with the definition of need from the beginning of any assessment project.

Making Recommendations Based on Your Assessment

The final step of most needs assessments is to make recommendations (or decisions) about what should happen next. The definition of need influences key decisions you have to make in this step—from what alternatives get considered to how data are used to support recommendations. When presenting recommendations based on a discrepancy definition (Table 2.1), you would directly link a proposed solution (or solutions) to the closing of the discrepancy. To do this, you might furthermore choose to use a multi-criteria analysis (Watkins et al., 2012) in order to compare alternatives and prioritize options.

New Directions for Evaluation • DOI: 10.1002/ev

In contrast, if you use a goals definition with motivational drivers of behavior (Maslow's hierarchy), then the focus may be on individual aspirations and how they can best be supported. These recommendations might come from a survey or other data to reflect the values of participants. Next steps in this context might stress on creating an environment where people are intrinsically motivated to achieve organizational objectives. The definition of need influences recommendations and decisions arising from a needs assessment.

Summary

There is nothing so practical as a good theory. Kurt Lewin (1951, p. 169)

Our goal was to rekindle a professional dialogue about what is a need (and thereby, what is a needs assessment). The chapter begins with a case for the importance of a clear and consistent definition of needs as the guiding light for any needs assessment and evaluation for that matter. As Stockman (2011) posited, "there is broad consensus on the fact that evaluations must take into account the perspectives and needs of the stakeholders" (p. 36). Meyer (2011) furthered "evaluation by its definition has primary emphasis on 'usefulness' and its orientation towards the needs of clients and stake-holders" (p. 135).

With this as a foundation, a variety of meanings were offered (Table 2.1), along with a framework for thinking about the relationships embedded in the definitions. Lastly, the implications a selected definition of need would have on the design, implementation, and results of a needs assessment were examined.

We hope that there can be a professional debate in the coming years about what are needs, and needs assessment, and their role in practice. This is not to necessarily create broad consensus on a single definition, but rather to enhance the foundations of research and practice in the profession as well as those in disciplines carrying on similar debates. We recognize that defining needs may also limit, or set boundaries around, professional practice. This is not our intent, rather we want the discussion of needs to expand bringing in wants, assets, and other important considerations into the discourse.

To continue the dialogue, we encourage you to enter conversations about needs assessment at conferences, write articles sharing experiences, join us on social media (http://www.linkedin.com/groups/Needs-Assessment-4151483), and to start professional interactions about what is a "need" the next time an internal or external client requests a needs assessment (or an evaluation).

References

Altschuld, J. W., & Lepicki, T. L. (2010). Needs assessment in education. In P. Peterson, & E. Baker (Eds.), *The international encyclopedia of education* (3rd ed., pp. 786–791). Oxford, UK: Elsevier.

Anscombe, G. E. M. (1958/1981). Modern moral philosophy. In G. E. M. Anscombe (Ed.), *Ethics, religion and politics: Collected philosophical papers volume III* (pp. 26–42). Oxford, UK: Blackwell.

Atwood, H. M., & Ellis, J. (1971). The concept of need: An analysis for adult education. *Adult Leadership, 19*, 210–212.

Bradshaw, J. (1972). The concept of social need. *New Society, 19*(496), 640–643.

Brandt, T. (2011). The social context of evaluation. In R. Stockmann (Ed.), *A practitioner handbook on evaluation* (pp. 369–421). Cheltenham, UK: Edward Elgar.

Bremner, R. (1956). *From the depths: The discovery of poverty in the United States.* New York: New York University Press.

Brock, G. (2005). Needs and global justice. In S. Reader (Ed.), *The philosophy of need* (pp. 51–72). Cambridge, UK: Cambridge University Press.

Carroll, L. (1865). *Alice's adventures in wonderland.* London, UK: MacMillan.

Clarke, J., & Langan, M. (1998). Review. In M. Langan (Ed.), *Welfare: Needs, rights and risks* (pp. 259–271). London, UK: Routledge.

Doyal, L., & Gough, I. (1991). *A theory of human need.* New York, NY: MacMillan.

Frankfurt, H. (1998). Necessity and desire. In G. Brock (Ed.), *Necessary goods: Our responsibilities to meet others' needs* (pp. 19–32). Oxford, UK: Rowman and Littlefield.

Gough, I. (2002, September). *Lists and thresholds: Comparing the Doyal-Gough theory of human need with Nussbaum's capabilities approach.* Paper presented at the Conference on Promoting Women's Capabilities: Examining Nussbaum's Capabilities Approach, St. Edmund's College, Cambridge, UK.

Greenwald, H. (1975). *Direct decision therapy.* San Diego, CA: Edits Publishing.

Gupta, K., Sleezer, C., & Russ-Eft, D. (2007). *A practical guide to needs assessment* (2nd ed.). San Francisco, CA: Pfeiffer.

Hamilton, L. A. (2003). *The political philosophy of needs.* Cambridge, UK: Cambridge University Press.

Hamilton, L. A. (2006). The context and argument of the political philosophy of needs (Symposium on The Political Philosophy of Needs). *The South African Journal of Philosophy, 25*(3), 224–232.

Kaufman, R. (1996). *Strategic thinking: A guide to identifying and solving problems.* Arlington, VA: American Society for Training & Development and the International Society for Performance Improvement.

Kaufman, R. (2011). *A manager's pocket guide to strategic thinking and planning.* Amherst, MA: HRD Press.

Kaufman, R., & Guerra-Lopez, I. (2013). *Needs assessment for organizational success.* Alexandria, VA: ASTD Press.

Lewin, K. (1946). Action research and minority problems. *Journal of Social Issues, 2*(4), 34–46.

Lewin, K. (1951). Problems of research in social psychology. In D. Cartwright (Ed.), *Field theory in social science: Selected theoretical papers* (pp. 155–169). New York, NY: Harper & Row.

Lister, R. (2010). *Understanding theories and concepts in social policy.* Bristol, UK: Policy Press.

Mallmann, C. A., & Marcus, S. (1980). Logical clarifications in the study of needs. In K. Lederer (Ed.), *Human needs: A contribution to the current debate* (pp. 163–185). Cambridge, MA: Oelgeschlager, Gunn & Hain.

Maslow, A. H. (1943). A theory of human motivation. *Psychological Review, 50*(4), 370–396.

Maslow, A. H. (1970a). *Motivation and personality*. New York, NY: Harper & Row.

Maslow, A. H. (1970b). *Religions, values, and peak experiences*. New York, NY: Penguin.

Max-Neef, M. A., Elizalde, A., & Hopenhayn, M. (1991). *Human scale development*. New York, NY: The Apex Press.

McCain, R. (2011). Why need is "An Idea We Cannot Do Without" in economics. Retrieved from http://faculty.lebow.drexel.edu/mccainr/top/eco/wps/needs.pdf

McLeod, S. K. (2011). Knowledge of need. *International Journal of Philosophical Studies*, *19*(2), 211–230.

Meyer, W. (2011). Evaluation designs. In R. Stockmann (Ed.), *A practitioner handbook on evaluation* (pp. 135–157). Cheltenham, UK: Edward Elgar.

Monette, M. (1979). Need assessment: A critique of philosophical assumptions. *Adult Education Quarterly*, *29*(2), 83–95.

Nutt, P. (2008). Investigating the success of decision making processes. *Journal of Management Studies*, *45*(2), 425–455.

Reader, S. (2005). Introduction. In S. Reader (Ed.), *The philosophy of need* (pp. 1–24). Cambridge, UK: Cambridge University Press.

Rossett, A. (1989). Assess for success. *Training and Development*, *43*(5), 55–59.

Rossett, A. (1995). Needs assessment. In G. Anglin (Ed.), *Instructional technology: Past, present, and future* (2nd ed., pp. 183–196). Englewood, CO: Libraries Unlimited.

Ryan, R. M., & Deci, E. L. (2000). The darker and brighter sides of human existence: Basic psychological needs as a unifying concept. *Psychological Inquiry*, *11*, 319–338.

Smith, A. (1776). *An inquiry into the nature and causes of the wealth of nations*. Chicago, IL: University of Chicago Press.

Stockman, R. (2011). An introduction to evaluation. In. R. Stockmann (Ed.), *A practitioner handbook on evaluation* (pp. 13–51). Cheltenham, UK: Edward Elgar.

Tracy, L. (1983). Basic human needs: A living systems perspective. In G. E. Laske (Ed.), *The relation between major world problems and systems learning* (pp. 595–601). Seaside, CA: Intersystems.

Triner, D., Greenberry, A., & Watkins, R. (1996). Training needs assessment: A contradiction in terms. *Educational Technology*, *36*(6), 51–55.

von Bertalanffy, L. (1969). *General system theory*. New York, NY: George Braziller.

Watkins, R., West Meiers, M., & Visser, Y. (2012). *A guide to assessing needs: Essential tools for collecting information, making decisions, and achieving development results*. Washington, DC: The World Bank.

Wiggins, D. (1987). Needs, need, needing. *Journal of Medical Ethics*, *13*, 62–68.

Wiggins, D. (2005). An idea we cannot do without. In S. Reader (Ed.), *The philosophy of need* (pp. 25–50). Cambridge, UK: Cambridge University Press.

Witkin, B. R. (1984). *Assessing needs in educational and social programs*. San Francisco, CA: Jossey-Bass.

Wright, J., Williams, R., & Wilkinson, J. R. (1998). The development of health needs assessment. In J. Wright (Ed.), *The development of health needs assessment in practice* (pp. 1–11). London, UK: BMJ Books.

RYAN WATKINS *is an associate professor at George Washington University in Washington, DC, and founder of www.NeedsAssessment.org and www.WeShareScience.com.*

JOLANTA KAVALE *is an independent performance consultant, lecturer, and head of Career Centre at Kaunas University of Technology in Lithuania.*

NEW DIRECTIONS FOR EVALUATION • DOI: 10.1002/ev

Engle, M., & Altschuld, J. W. (2014). Needs assessment: The perspective from the public sector. In J. W. Altschuld & R. Watkins (Eds.), *Needs assessment: Trends and a view toward the future. New Directions for Evaluation, 144,* 33–45.

3

Needs Assessment: The Perspective From the Public Sector

Molly Engle, James W. Altschuld

Abstract

While examining needs is common in many public-sector agencies, questions arise about how it has been carried out and if a focus on deficits (or gaps) is too narrow when not accompanied by the assessment of assets. The authors operate in this chapter as actors in a play. The first author offers a short personal perspective about her long experience in the public sector, with emphasis on Extension and the nature of needs assessment within it. In that discussion are two illuminative historical examples with clear relevance to what we might do today. They demonstrate that linking asset-thinking to such efforts might be a good thing when embarking upon improvement of programs for the public. The second author enters in by amplifying the examination of assets and how they might be linked to the thinking of public-sector assessors. The authors conclude by recommending that such an expansion of the toolkit of needs assessors would be useful. © Wiley Periodicals, Inc., and the American Evaluation Association.

Introduction

To put this chapter into a context, let me start by telling you a little about *my story* (the Engle side) with *needs assessment*. For the last 30+ years, I have been an academic in a public-sector role, the public sector being one that receives some support from state/federal governments. In this role, I have had the opportunity to serve as an *internal evaluator*, a *program planner*, and a *classroom teacher*. Among other things, I have been asked to evaluate externally funded programs, internally funded programs, programs of my own design without additional funding (no easy task), and programs designed by others (with and without external funding). On several occasions, I have had to retrofit (design and implement an evaluation after the program has been conducted) program evaluations as well as design program evaluations. For many of you, this diversity of roles will sound familiar; my perception is that this is common among evaluators.

Only rarely, however, has my help been sought for straight-up needs assessments. I find that odd because a *needs assessment* is the first activity evaluators can and should undertake, especially at the start of programs and projects. After all, needs assessment can guide the many design, implementation, and evaluation decisions that follow. Given that a needs-based approach to problems is so engrained in the public-sector thinking, it is easy to get disenchanted with it. However, needs assessments are said to be done on a regular basis by many in the public sector. While this situation appears contradictory on several levels, I believe that my story and experiences in Extension service assessments can help shed some light on the practical value of assessment in the public sector (especially when assets are also integrated in the approach).

Background

To be effective, public-sector programs in Extension service, healthcare, public health, education, social service programs, marketing, policy development, and others must have a strong foundation; that foundation is needs assessment. Ideally, programs are identified and then developed only after a thorough assessment has been done particularly of the current condition or status. This is especially important for programs that are offered to and affect the public. But the reality is that programs are often undertaken without that needs assessment foundation, such as when they are the result of political deals or when a solution is selected before the needs are well defined and understood.

The skills and tools of a social scientist (evaluation being a social science) are key to doing needs assessment work. They include identification of appropriate stakeholders; delineation of the nature of the problem or issue in consideration; prioritizing issues, identifying underlying causes of problems, and hence, potentially illuminating variables to which resources should be directed; solicitation of possible solutions; and using the data from the process to inform decision making. The skills extend to evaluating programs and new initiatives that have come about as a result of doing the upfront work and are consistent with what Witkin and Altschuld (1995) suggest would be required for conducting needs assessment. Yet in my experience, this rarely happens in Extension services (Extension), and I find

Figure 3.1. Linear Logic Model (University of Wisconsin Extension Service)

Program Action - Logic Model

Inputs	Outputs		Outcomes - Impact		
	Activities	Participation	Short Term	Medium Term	Long Term

Situation	Priorities	What we invest	What we do	Who we reach	What the short term results are	What the medium term results are	What the ultimate impact(s) is
Situation	Consider:	What we invest	Conduct workshops, meetings	Participants			
Needs and assets	Mission	Staff	Deliver services	Clients	Learning	Action	Conditions
	Vision	Volunteers	Develop products, curriculum, resources	Agencies	Awareness	Behavior	Social
Symptoms versus problems	Values	Time	Train	Decision-makers	Knowledge	Practice	Economic
	Mandates	Money	Provide counseling	Customers	Attitudes	Decision-making	Civic
Stakeholder engagement	Resources	Research base	Assess		Skills		Environmental
	Collaborators	Materials	Facilitate	Satisfaction	Opinions	Policies	
	Competitors	Equipment	Partner		Aspirations	Social Action	
	Intended outcomes	Technology	Work with media		Motivations		
		Partners					

Assumptions	External Factors

Evaluation
Focus - Collect Data - Analyze and Interpret - Report

this odd because needs assessment and asset building are the first things that ought to be implemented when an issue comes to the table.

Extension programs are frequently simplified using a logic model approach. Typically those models are linear (Figure 3.1), though they may be circular. Looking at a linear logic model, the *situation* (at the far left) is the place where needs assessment occurs. In a circular program model, there may be no specific "situation" identified; rather, alternatives for a "situation" exist. So assessment is a task that is included in conceptualizing projects, activities, and their evaluations regardless of the logic model used, and it can provide a valid foundation on which to design a realistic logic model. Sometimes, but not as often, a needs assessment is done after the program has been implemented—perhaps identifying the audience or the activities, or whether the intended group did in fact use services and events provided for them, and how new variations may be more effective. Nowhere in these schemas do assets usually get mentioned (Altschuld, 2014), though they can be a valuable enabler for needs assessments.

Altschuld and Witkin (2000) noted that occasionally potential program users reject the current program because there is no need; because the questions were not asked to elicit the current situation; or, in the extreme, because the target audience does not see value in the service to be offered. In these instances, potential program participants simply do not participate, are not willing, or are adverse to the program that is made available. This situation is troubling, but it has been observed in both educational and health settings. Integrating assets, often including programs currently valued and being used by target participants, can improve the appetite for a closer examination of needs.

Figure 3.1 is an example of a prototypical logic model used by Extension services in the United States. In it, assets might come after the "situation" but less attention seems to be paid to them. Assets appear to be only superficial rather than a fully explored aspect of the context of the logic model. Perhaps, Extension could benefit from exploring these more, and in doing so make needs assessment more applicable to programming.

What You Find in the Literature

A cursory examination of literature is a useful starting place for getting a sense of the dissemination of information about needs assessment as used in Extension. The literature is replete with illustrations and applications in Extension, likely more so than in other public sectors. Within the last 10 years, for example, there have been over 200 articles in the *Journal of Extension* with needs assessment in the title or abstract (using the search terms needs+assessment+2003+2013). Modifying the search to the *American Journal of Evaluation* surfaced only two articles (none were returned with the additional key words); 361 articles were found in *Evaluation and Program Planning* for all fields using "needs assessment." The first journal covers Extension programs in the public sector; the last two report evaluation findings, with needs assessment seen as a subset of the broader evaluation field. Some disparity would be expected between the journals (one deals with programs more and the others address evaluations). Using a similar search and the terms "needs+assessment+assets+2003," the *Journal of Extension* returned 151 articles. It is important to emphasize that there is no journal devoted specifically to assessment, nor is there a source for gathering information on how assets are integrated (if at all); thus, resources are scattered throughout these journals and potentially those of other professional fields (such as training and performance improvement).

Needs assessment is clearly a topic of interest to authors, editors, and readers of the *Journal of Extension*; assets receive some but not much attention. Most of the articles that include *assets* talk about them only in terms of economics (mainly monetary resources available to the public/individual). Some deal with positive youth development and minimizing risk behaviors. Still others (and this is more tied to building capacity, called *asset assessment*) relate to the skills, knowledge, behaviors, and programs that currently exist in the community or individual, and are not being used (Adams, Place, & Swisher, 2009; Mathie & Cunningham, 2003). Mathie and Cunningham (2003) wrote of the "stronger, accountable forms of governance at the local level and the emergence of effective ... organizations" (p. 474). It is unclear from the article if these governance forms will focus on assets, continue to look more at needs, or deal with both entities.

New Directions for Evaluation • DOI: 10.1002/ev

The literature from the public sector leans heavily on case study applications, offering guidance of what to do and what not to do for those charged with implementing a needs assessment. This has been particularly useful to Extension service, though at times it has led to the replication of ineffective approaches and minimal integration of assets.

Needs Assessment and Extension

Although I have worked in varied fields, what is explained below is based on my (Engle) work with the Extension service and a sampling of what was found in the literature. First, a little background about the Extension service, often called the Cooperative Extension Service because of the cooperative funding streams. Extension is "a land-grant university-based outreach and educational organization" (Franz & Townson, 2008, p. 5) in every U.S. state and territory. The Morrill Act of 1862 established the land-grant universities, and there are today the "1862," the "1890," and the "1994" institutions based on the date of the legislation that designated them as such. The 1914 Smith–Lever Act established the Extension service with funds to provide community audiences (i.e., the public) research-based information in nontraditional educational settings. Historically, the Extension service has programming in food and nutrition, community development, natural resources (agriculture, forestry, and water-related topics), and 4-H youth development, with agriculture and forestry research stations (often called "other state-wide agencies") working with it.

In the 21st century, the Extension service moved into recycling, energy efficiency, and other areas responsive to changing dimensions of our society. Emerging programs may include topics such as marine coasts, invasive species, energy use and misuse, disaster preparedness, and/or climate chaos, depending on the locale and the target audience. Programs are located in diverse urban and rural settings and are aligned with the times. Whereas agriculture was once the focus, today programming embraces a broad array of topics.

The structure of the service varies from state to state, county to county, and, of necessity, must deal with a wide spread of internal and external constituencies with interests related to actual services to be rendered. (For an in-depth discussion see Braverman, Engle, Arnold, & Rennekamp, 2008.) Content specialists are state-level faculty and Extension educators (also called field faculty or agents) who serve the county or region. These two groups (specialists and field faculty) are responsible for developing programs. Some of what they do is content related (cereal crops, recycling, or another area) and other efforts arise from trends (rainwater gardens, permeable ground covers), increased frequency of public occurrence (invasive species), or skills of the specialist (weeds, demography).

In the terminology of needs assessment (Witkin & Altschuld, 1995), the programs are at Level 1 (individuals or groups requiring assistance or help) or Level 2 (individuals who provide a service, such as teachers, health-care providers, Extension professionals, and similar personnel). Most often, the Extension service will not invest in programs unless there is a demand for them generated from the ground up (stated by the target audience, such as related to cereal crops) or top down (skills necessary to do the job, conflicts of interest).

In a perfect world, needs assessments establish direction—with that direction being different from county to county, region to region, and state-to-state. Sometimes the process is neat and well done, and at others it operates on the squeaky wheel principle (those that complain get resources). Caravella (2006) in an article titled "A Needs Assessment Method for Extension Educators" describes a method to Extension educators for conducting a needs assessment using existing sources and information. She mentions that numerous procedures have been used to collect data (advisory boards, surveys, focus group interviews, key informant interviews). These processes may or may not be systematically implemented. Always the assessment is based on what the stakeholders perceive to be lacking and this may include what are called wants (more wishes or desires) than actual needs (Watkins & Kavale, Chapter 2 of this issue).

Nowhere do the approaches in her discussion nor do many other needs assessment methodologies talk about what IS in terms of assets, only what is NOT. From an interview with an Extension Administrator (D. Maddy, personal communication, January 23, 2014), I was able to learn when an assessment is conducted there is (typically) a "laundry list" of programs presented; nowhere are the stakeholders or the constituencies they represent asked what they already have in terms of services that Extension could support or augment. Stakeholders are only asked what they need/want/don't have, and their views or perceptions appear to be impetus for future programs. A full needs assessment (Witkin & Altschuld, 1995) would not have been implemented as in questions like:

- Have concrete discrepancies, between what is and what should be, been determined?
- Were discrepancies identified by a variety of methods with triangulation across them?
- Have discrepancies been prioritized for actions to be taken?
- Were concerns looked at with regard to the counterfactual state (what would happen if nothing were to be done, would some of them resolve themselves)?
- What are the risk factors of not attending to a need been considered in terms of costs?
- Have political risks been taken into account?
- What is the number of people affected by meeting or not meeting a need or multiple needs been identified?

- Did easy-to-resolve needs guide decisions as opposed to the harder, more long term, intransigent needs?
- Have programs and efforts put in place to resolve needs actually been evaluated as to their impact and effectiveness in accord with the short-term and long-term features on logic maps?

Next are cases illustrating needs assessment in Extension.

One Example From the Extension Service

A "needs assessment" that was implemented by the Extension service with which I (Engle) am familiar was designed for strategic guidance for future programming and developing a legislative funding package. The process deliberately focused on where Extension should invest new funds and what shifts in staff that might be needed as attrition happens. The county level administrators (stakeholders) were asked to assist in the process by providing logistical support at the county level. The expected outcomes were to provide a practical vision of the preferred future for Extension and a prioritized list of the most important issues and *needs* of the specific jurisdiction in consideration. An issue was defined as an area of concern or challenge; a need was defined by what was lacking, or what was wanted. Surprisingly, although each county was involved in the process, the needs assessment resulted only in a state-wide report coming from county data.

Stakeholders were individuals visible in the county, such as commissioners, legislators, industry leaders, civic groups, and possible new audiences. By inviting them to focus groups, it was anticipated that the audience would have a good grasp of local circumstances and needs. Extension faculty members and staff were not the target audience, but they had the opportunity to observe the interviews in an unobtrusive way so as to not bias the responses of interview participants.

The concern for Extension Administration was developing a meaningful package that could be used to develop new programs as well as by the legislature for funding. So while a state-wide report was the desired outcome, there was the question how can data be disaggregated for county use. "Needs" expressed by water-stressed counties would be different from those from wet counties and so on with regard to urban or rural counties, metropolitan or nonmetropolitan counties, eastern or western counties, and agriculture-based or non-agriculture-based counties. The diversity of concerns presented by varied constituencies is vast, and making sure that counties were represented in a meaningful state-wide report was challenging.

The level of possible programming is also challenging for the Extension service. The frequency of a stated "need" could result in a state-wide program or in a county-level program. If the vocal minority voiced a "need" and the silent majority didn't offer an alternative, did that mean that this was truly a "need"? If the "need" frequency was such that it called for programming state-wide, yet it was geographically tied to the eastern or western part of the state, does that really reflect a state-wide need? If the frequency was such that it occurred only in a few counties scattered across the state (in both eastern and western parts), does that really reflect a county-wide "need"? These are issues that the Extension service must grapple with continually.

Additionally, the service receives a good portion of its funding from the state and those resources are limited by the state budget. Balancing state-wide and county-wide priorities with fiscal and personnel resources is an ongoing problem and is accomplished through a vetted process involving key stakeholders within Extension Administration and counties; individual personal favorite programs are not necessarily those that receive limited resources.

Even though there was a careful process applied to the choice of programming, not everyone was happy with the outcome (which is common for needs assessments). County staff were advised that not every need identified could be addressed (cost, personnel, and other factors) but that the collection of needs would be taken into account once the meetings were over. Outputs of the focus groups were summarized and shared with the *total Extension faculty* (emphasis added) for reactions and input into a Strategic Directions Workshop later in the year. What came from that meeting was likewise shared with ALL Extension faculty members, staff, and other county-based stakeholders. From there a legislative package was developed with accompanying budget.

The package was developed from a state-wide process with an agenda to demonstrate to the legislature that state-wide agencies had a greater need than covered by the current proposed budget. Thus, politics may have clouded true needs and obfuscated the issues and concerns—again, a common occurrence in many needs assessments. It is important to note that there are covert political forces that weigh heavily on outcomes. This is typical of what the Extension service must deal with and often leads to questions about true need.

Other Examples—Extension and Aging

My (Engle, the first author) experience is that needs assessment can identify unmet needs, provide evidence of community support, and increase public involvement. Frequently, it provides community members with a way to express strong opinions on issues or to get their voices to be heard. Note what took place in the following examples and how assets can become a valuable part of thinking about needs.

In Florida, the Extension service combined a survey-based needs assessment with community service learning, involving the youth of the community (Israel & Ilvento, 1995). This effort was an opportunity to enhance the development of concerned citizens in the community, namely youth, and to accomplish another objective—saving funds. Local schools provided the labor, expertise in computers, and potential participants, the location in which to conduct the survey as well as students. Students collected data and provided help to the community in clarifying needs. It is believed that by so doing they experienced a deeper sense of the community, its development and enhancement.

This approach created collaborations where previously there were none. Students helped write the questions and design the survey. Likewise, citizen participation was solicited by slogans generated by the students. The students were also trained to do interviews and actually conducted over half of them. This is akin to rapid appraisal techniques used in ascertaining needs. The survey provided information about "needs," had scientific rigor, and maximized community involvement. The local leaders initiated the project with the idea that getting into the heart of the community was critical. The survey implementation came from a positive vision of the assets (i.e., students and their skills) available through the schools.

The second, and much earlier case, deals with aging and contains principles that still resonate today. The Alabama Commission on Aging and the University of Alabama (UAB) Center for Aging conducted a face-to-face interview of a random sample of individuals 55 and over in 13 counties in Alabama (Hughes, Engle, & Caldwell, 1987). This was only a subset of Alabama's 67 counties, but the data matched results from a state-wide survey carried out 15 years back. Over 1,000 respondents were interviewed from metropolitan and nonmetropolitan counties to determine the current status of Alabama's elderly and their needs.

A large number of individuals throughout the state were utilized to gather interview data, with significant time being devoted to training them as mandated by the protocol for the study. The interviewers were instructed to try to understand interviewees without showing reaction to their comments or influencing them in any way. In addition, there were three other goals for the interview process: (a) communicating the importance of the respondents' views, (b) indicating that there are no right or wrong answers to questions, and (c) ensuring that respondents felt that they were making valuable contributions to research and/or service.

Prior to the availability of electronic communications, initial contact was made with respondents using paper forms or by phone. This study indicated that face-to-face contact was more effective than mail or phone contact. (Today, consents are more often electronic but for some groups face to face may still be best.) Personal interaction was critical due to the fact that the interview could take up to two hours and every question had be asked; skipping them could lead to an incomplete picture of the status of aging.

Besides demographics, this survey gathered information on health, health risks, psychosocial well-being, daily living activities, environmental status, and awareness of social services. Data summaries were used to identify areas where the citizens' needs were not being met. Agencies were then responsible for developing programs to meet them. A significant conclusion was that many of the respondents reported the "assets" that contributed to their quality of living. What were anticipated as problems did not materialize (lack of services) while other areas did (access to service). Assets were built into the interview process, but not specifically labeled as such. Respondents were allowed to focus on individual situations rather than specifically addressing generalized community needs or assets.

Although this study is from the late 1980s, it shows how respondents choose to talk about assets when the interviewer was specifically seeking "needs" from the discrepancy perspective. It appears that the respondents wanted the interviewers to know that being "old" didn't necessarily imply that something was lacking in their lives (needs), rather what was present was just as important (perhaps more so) as what was missing. Although not recognized at the time, this survey demonstrated how the target community viewed its strengths and focused on them, and that perceived "needs" were not needed. Strengths of the community supported the respondents, and the Center on Aging was potentially imposing a cognitive bias on what it was investigating.

Collectively in these last two examples a subtle point is evident. Needs and asset assessment are being done in the public sector (and have been for some time) but they take on many different shapes and forms. And even articles and reports about such assessments may not identify them using today's terminology.

Glass Half Full; Glass Half Empty

So what is a "need" in the context of public institutions like Extension? Is true *need* about what is lacking or about what is present? Does a needs assessment fully make sense for improving lives if we only think about a need as a deficit? Does this constrain our vision and narrow our assessments too much?

Altschuld (the coauthor) reenters the discourse by stressing the philosophical stance of gaps (needs) as opposed to assets, that is, a deficit definition of need can connote a negative viewpoint (focusing on the empty half of the glass), whereas when thinking about assets a positive perception is apparent (the half full glass). The idea is that starting out with needs underscores the lack of something instead of the presence of something. In his 2014 book, he shows that beginning with needs may not lead to good new programming, whereas launching efforts from assets may indeed provide a more complete picture and improved results.

This principle (building from assets as opposed to needs) was observed in a study about curbing gun violence (Altschuld, 2014). It employed a coalition to set up a program to stop or lower the use of weapons. In another case, investigators took advantage of a radio station to bring out the voice of the people and as way to include community members in the delivery of services. This illuminated the almost hidden resources and strengths the community possessed and that had not been thought about much. Most of this would not have happened if the initial premise was that of needs, deficits.

Initiatives such as just discussed, and some of those given earlier, are actually reflective of a hybrid approach of asset-based capacity building and needs assessment (Altschuld, Hung, & Lee, Chapter 7 of this issue). In every circumstance, assets were the foundation and governing philosophy for thinking about improvement as tempered by an understanding of needs. Neither needs assessment nor an asset approach can operate and make sense in a vacuum devoid of the other. A balance is necessary for resolving complex social problems, by themselves they are not up to the task but a hybrid position is (the glass is both half full and half empty at the same time).

Assets set the picture more comprehensively (looking at what is present and what the target audience brings to the table); at the same time, many individuals and groups are attuned to what is NOT present (need, discrepancy, gap) as opposed to what IS (asset, resource, strength). The latter seems to be done less often and people are perhaps more conditioned to see needs rather than how their strengths can affect situations.

Throughout all the examples here, and in the 2014 book, a hybrid approach requires longer implementation and more resources (dollars, human skills, etc.). We suggest that resolving serious problems in society and institutions more than compensates for the extra time and resources. This leads to the question why haven't we seen more hybrid approaches in the public sector (where complex societal issues are supposed to be addressed) regardless of its greater upfront costs?

This finding could be explained in several ways. Viewing the picture comprehensively is more than asking stakeholders to articulate what issue is important; it involves asking them what is available (assets). Every stakeholder in a community can delineate existing strengths but more than likely they have not been asked about them. Simultaneously recognize that they are more used to talking about what is lacking rather than what is present. Is the glass half full (assets) or half empty (deficits)? It is both and you should assess both.

The hybrid approach raises numerous questions for evaluators, such as:

- What are the organizational, service, and social groups that add strength to the community?
- What other groups (police, fire personnel, healthcare providers, churches, sporting groups) could be involved?
- What kinds of connections (networks), formal or informal, exist or might exist across organizations that might be the bedrock for change? Extension reaches out to partners, engaging the community; this would be an opportunity to demonstrate that.

NEW DIRECTIONS FOR EVALUATION • DOI: 10.1002/ev

- How has the community worked together in the past to improve relationships and provide services? How could this be done today and in the future?
- What is the community spirit—cooperation, isolation, coordination—that can be built and used to the advantage of the community?
- What are the skills of individuals in our communities—youth, adult, seniors? What resources do these groups have?
- What assistance can those skills provide?
- What can community individuals do to help in facilitating activities?
- How can schools and other educational institutions contribute?
- How can local businesses and establishments contribute? This could be as simple as places for people to meet about local issues or perhaps having small discounts on goods and services for local participants.

Lessons Learned

Given much of what has been said so far, you might conclude that needs assessments in the public sector are largely contrived based on personal or political agendas. It is likely that organizations (Extension, public health, education) identify what is lacking so they can resolve gaps with solutions they already have in mind (admittedly a cynical perspective of the public sector). Or, more optimistically, perhaps there is just a lack of awareness of what can be achieved from a broad participatory approach to needs assessment that integrates assets into the mix.

In the context of public-sector needs assessment, it would likely make sense to focus more, though not exclusively, on where the strengths lie. Devoting time to the study and experiment with assets and needs should be done to develop programming based on consensus.

Conducting a needs assessment is costly. There are training, travel, marketing, and other costs associated with gaining the input of multiple stakeholders groups. They may (and probably do) have personal agendas that they want to address and which may (or may not) speak to the needs of the community. That being said, conducting a systematic assessment of needs and assets for that matter is critical for programs which will provide the community with skills that are currently not existing or only minimally existing. The community is a rich source of direction; needs assessment with assets embedded can capture that richness.

References

Adams, A. E., Place, N. T., & Swisher, M. E. (2009). Knowledge levels regarding the concept of community food security among Florida Extension agents. *Journal of Extension, 47*(4). Retrieved from http://www.joe.org/joe/2009august/rb2.php

Altschuld, J. W. (2014). *Bridging the gap between asset/capacity building and needs assessment: Concepts and practical applications.* Thousand Oaks, CA: Sage.

New Directions for Evaluation • DOI: 10.1002/ev

Altschuld, J. W., & Engle, M. (2013, October). *Needs assessment and asset capacity building: Linking the concepts.* Professional development workshop presented at the annual meeting of the American Evaluation Association, Washington, DC.

Altschuld, J. W., & Witkin, B. R. (2000). *From needs assessment to action: Transforming needs into solution strategies.* Thousand Oaks, CA: Sage.

Braverman, M. T., Engle, M., Arnold, M. E., & Rennekamp, R. A. (Eds.). (2008). *New Directions for Evaluation: No. 120. Program evaluation in a complex organizational system: Lessons from Cooperative Extension.* San Francisco, CA: Jossey-Bass.

Caravella, J. (2006). A needs assessment method for Extension educators. *Journal of Extension, 44*(1). Retrieved from http://www.joe.org/joe/2006february/tt2p.shtml

Franz, N. K., & Townson, L. (2008). The nature of complex organizations: The case of Cooperative Extension. *New Directions for Evaluation, 120,* 5–14.

Hughes, G. H., Engle, M., & Caldwell, J. A. (1987). *Statewide survey of Alabama's Elderly.* Birmingham, AL: UAB Center for Aging.

Israel, G. D., & Ilvento, T. W. (1995). Everybody wins: Involving youth in community needs assessment. *Journal of Extension, 33*(2). Retrieved from http://www.joe.org/joe/1995april/al.php

Mathie, A., & Cunningham, G. (2003). From clients to citizens: Asset-based community development as a strategy for community-driven development. *Development in Practice, 13*(5), 474–486. Retrieved from http://www.coloradocollege.edu/dotAsset/27454fab-98e8-4d89-80a0-044837593aa0.pdf

Witkin, B. R., & Altschuld, J. W. (1995). *Planning and conducting needs assessments: A practical guide.* Thousand Oaks, CA: Sage.

MOLLY ENGLE *is professor in the College of Education, the Extension Service evaluation specialist at Oregon State University, and past-president of the American Evaluation Association.*

JAMES W. ALTSCHULD *is professor emeritus in the College of Education and Human Ecology, The Ohio State University.*

NEW DIRECTIONS FOR EVALUATION • DOI: 10.1002/ev

Wedman, J. (2014). Needs assessments in the private sector. In J. W. Altschuld & R. Watkins (Eds.), *Needs assessment: Trends and a view toward the future. New Directions for Evaluation*, 144, 47–60.

4

Needs Assessments in the Private Sector

John Wedman

Abstract

While needs assessments are clearly embedded in education and social pro-grams, assessments are also a long-standing tradition in business and industry. A needs assessment is conducted to enhance organizational development and improve individual and group performance. This chapter includes a short his-tory of needs assessment in the private sector context and brief examples of its use in identifying solutions that will improve performance and business results. Wedman's Performance Pyramid is used as the framework for examining se-lected examples. The chapter closes with discussions of how to "sell" the needs assessment and performance improvement process, and how needs assessment and evaluation are linked. © Wiley Periodicals, Inc., and the American Evaluation Association.

Background

Determining when the idea of "needs assessment" first surfaced is an im-possible task. No doubt, someone during the Stone Age figured out what was required to improve hunters' performance when using a stone axe. For some reason, I doubt a training seminar was high on the lists of performance improvement solutions.

John wrote about and conducted needs assessments since well before the turn of the 21st century, and this volume is dedicated in his memory.

NEW DIRECTIONS FOR EVALUATION, no. 144, Winter 2014 © 2014 Wiley Periodicals, Inc., and the American Evaluation Association. Published online in Wiley Online Library (wileyonlinelibrary.com) • DOI: 10.1002/ev.20102

Fast forward about four-to-six thousand years, and we find Mager and Pipe (1970) offering their first edition of *Analyzing Performance Problems, or, You Really Oughta Wanna.* This short book (112 pp.) provides a procedure for examining performance problems and suggesting the direction that will lead to solutions for resolution. A short time later, Harless wrote about "front-end analysis," a term that is more or less related to "needs assessment." In 1973, he said:

> Front-end analysis is about money, first and foremost. It's about how to spend money in ways that will be most beneficial to the organization and the performers in that organization. It's also about avoiding spending money on silly things like instruction when there is no instructional problem; or training everybody in everything when you can get by with training fewer people in a few things; or flying lots of trainees in for a course when a send-out checklist would do. (p. 229)

Avoiding the debate about the differences and similarities between front-end analysis and needs assessment, a cursory look at Harless' quote clearly indicates he viewed the former in the context of private sector organizations where money is a driving force and is increasingly strong in the public sector today.

In 1978, Gilbert published his seminal work, *Human Competence: Engineering Worthy Performance.* It introduced the Behavior Engineering Model (BEM); BEM provided what was considered at the time to be a comprehensive perspective for diagnosing performance problems. The model included several interrelated factors that, when present and adequate, result in increased performance.

Gilbert argued that the root of most performance problems could be found in the environment rather than in the individual performer. Thus, the needs assessment process begins with an examination of barriers in the environment (such as lack of instruments or incentives) and later progresses to an examination of barriers in the individual (such as lack of knowledge or capacity).

Mager, Harless, and Gilbert laid the foundation for many variations and improvements in approaches to needs assessment for performance improvement. Today, there are many books, periodicals, websites, and other media forms that focus on the topic.

Placed in content, needs assessment is a subset of human performance technology (HPT). HPT can be thought of as the process of identifying performance needs, implementing solutions to meet these needs, and evaluating the impact of the solutions on performance and the resulting outcomes. In comparison, needs assessment is used to identify performance needs and to make recommendations about potential solutions. HPT goes beyond the recommendations and to implementing solutions and evaluating their impact. How is the needs assessment process typically carried out in business practices?

Common Business Practices

While based primarily on anecdotal evidence and personal experience, most businesses are not particularly adept at assessing their needs in order to improve performance. In 1999, Gayeski noted that, "...many training and human resources professionals have found it very difficult to make the transition from their traditional roles to the more comprehensive HPT (human performance technology) roles." She rightly pointed out that many practitioners want to apply HPT in their jobs, but they cannot. Rossett and Czech (1995) found that while most practitioners were confident of their skills regarding performance technology in general and needs assessment in particular, they felt limited to influence implementation of the HPT process.

Lacking the influence within the organization to conduct a comprehensive needs assessment and implement the solutions derived from the finding, practitioners end up conducting a "wants assessment" which asks, What do performers and their supervisors want to do or have others do? The "wants" are frequently lacking in terms of data, opting to rely more on personal opinion and ill-founded assumptions. The end results are all too often characterized by limited impact on performance and minimal impact on business outcomes.

What's Missing?

In addition to lacking the influence (and likely the culture in the business setting) required for conducting a comprehensive needs assessment, practitioners are saddled with two other challenges. First, to be valued, a needs assessment must link the data that were gathered and analyzed to the drivers (i.e., priorities) of the organization's business model. For example, a high-tech company that has "innovation" as a priority may be less interested in improving efficiency and more interested in building knowledge assets (acquiring patents, expanding R&D). In this case, a needs assessment focusing on efficient operations is not likely to play well in a company driven by innovation.

The second challenge facing practitioners is that many of the performance improvement models are overly complex, lack a systemic perspective, and/or are too mechanistic to be of value. This is discussed next, followed by examples of needs assessment projects that addressed the challenge.

Simple, Systemic, and Organic Needs Assessment

Performance improvement and needs assessment are not necessarily complex. In fact, one might argue that both concepts are common sense—if you want to improve performance, figure out why the performance is not producing the desired accomplishment. Looking a little deeper, a *simple* observation becomes evident: In order to accomplish something of significance, three factors must be in place: vision, resources, and support system. By extension, the needs assessment process makes it possible to determine which of these are not in place.

Having the right factors there entails two critical relationships: adequacy and alignment. Adequacy means having enough of what is required (a compelling vision, sufficient resources, and a support system that will enable the desired results to be accomplished). Alignment is that the factors are all pointing in the same direction (resources and the support structure are both committed to the vision). For example, a short-sighted or vaguely focused vision is likely not adequate. And a support system and resources that are dedicated to different visions are probably not aligned.

The elements making up the support system must also be adequate and aligned. As an illustration, consider a utility company that has the goal of reducing on-the-job injury, particularly back injuries resulting from moving heavy objects. A new tool might be part of the solution, provided there is an adequate supply of the tools. However, to achieve the injury-reduction goal, training must be modified (aligned) to include proper tool use, incentives should be in place to encourage use, and feedback regarding use should be provided. These and other relationships play out in a highly interrelated manner at many different layers and across multiple contexts, making for a *systemic* approach to needs assessment and performance improvement. If one of the elements is inadequate or not aligned with the other elements, performance will suffer.

Interestingly, Gayeski (1999) likened HPT to a tree and its interrelated parts (roots, trunk, branches). This *organic* perspective on HPT is fundamental to performance improvement and needs assessment. Early models in the field were often mechanistic and linear; equations (Gilbert) and flow charts (Mager) were commonplace. Not surprisingly, the mechanical/linear perspective seldom meshed well with the prevailing culture in most private sector organizations. Assembly lines were being replaced by assembly teams and "Japanese style management" was being substituted for the "command and control" mentality. A needs assessment process that is sensitive to the ever-changing, dynamic, and "messy" realities of organizations is more likely to be accepted and to be effective than earlier structures, particularly when organization culture and change processes are integral to performance improvement.

The lack of a simple, systemic, and organic needs assessment framework resulted in the development of Wedman's Performance Pyramid. (Due to other uses of the term "Performance Pyramid," it became necessary to add "Wedman's" to the title for clarity.)

NEW DIRECTIONS FOR EVALUATION • DOI: 10.1002/ev

Figure 4.1. Factors Enabling, or Impeding, Accomplishments

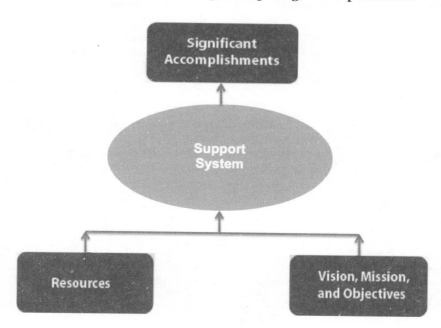

Wedman's Performance Pyramid

The Performance Pyramid has been described in several other publications (Steege, Marra, & Jones, 2012; Wedman, 2010) rendering a detailed description unnecessary so a brief overview will be provided. The Pyramid is grounded in the observation that in order to accomplish something of significance, vision, resources, and a support system are necessary. As depicted in Figure 4.1, they must work together to enable accomplishments.

For the support system, six interrelated elements are in play with their interactions critical to optimal performance (Table 4.1). Figure 4.2 offers greater detail with the addition of "change process," "continuous monitoring," and "organizational culture" to the perspective. As a note of clarification, the organizational culture (OC) component is shown as part of the support system. Metaphorically, OC is the "spice" that has an influence on each of the support system elements. While OC is not one of the elements, its influence extends well beyond any particular needs assessment and performance improvement effort.

When all elements of the support system are in place and linked with available resources and clear vision, significant accomplishments become likely. The needs assessment process is used to identify inadequate or misaligned elements and to generate potential solutions. For instance, a

Table 4.1. Support System Elements

Support System Elements	Description
Tools, environment, and processes	Ranging from a simple job aid to large equipment, tools are essential to optimal performance. The tools are applied in the work environment, where tangible and intangible features enable or impede performance. Processes are used to standardize and streamline performance.
Expectations and feedback	Knowing what level of performance is expected and receiving feedback on work-related activities shapes and focuses performance.
Reward, recognition, and incentives	Rewards, recognition, and incentives are used to facilitate changes in performance. These elements may be positive or negative, depending on the adequacy of the performance.
Performance capability	Performers must have the mental, social, and physical abilities to meet expectations? While some abilities can be developed over time, matching an individual's or group's ability to the performance task is considerably more efficient.
Motivation and self-concept	Whereas rewards, recognition, and incentives are external to the performer, motivation to perform and a positive self-concept are internal attributes. Individuals who do not want to meet expectations or do not view themselves as competent are very unlikely to demonstrate optimal performance.
Knowledge and skills	Optimal performers must have the know-how to meet expectations. Formal training and job experience build the necessary knowledge and skills. How do you differentiate this from performance capability—not a major concern and probably needs little amplification.

business that does not give performance feedback is likely to struggle. That was the case with one of my clients. Upper management was hesitant to provide corrective feedback to its production line leaders. Each leader was allowed to change how the production line was calibrated, which resulted in excessive downtime each time there was a shift change. For more details regarding Wedman's Performance Pyramid and the needs assessment process, please check out: NeedsAssessment.missouri.edu

The Pyramid in the Private Sector: Real Performance Problems and Solutions

The Pyramid framework has been applied in a wide variety of settings, ranging from K–12 schools to multinational corporations. The first two examples next focus on the private sector and the last one on a recent project in a military context. Each concludes with a few "lessons learned."

NEW DIRECTIONS FOR EVALUATION • DOI: 10.1002/ev

Figure 4.2. Complete Pyramid Framework

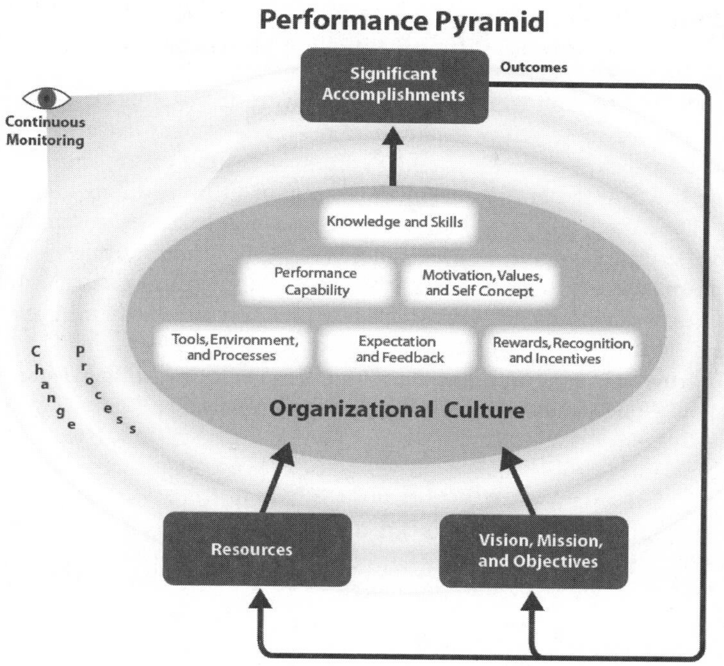

Performance Pyramid

Example 1: Flip-Flops in the Workplace

Imagine working at a nuclear power plant that is the source of electricity for over half a million people in a major metropolitan area: lots of heavy equipment, megawatts of electric current, and the ever-present danger of an emergency situation—not exactly the kind of workplace where employees would want to wear flip-flops, but some did according to their union representative. For a variety of reasons, plant management did not agree.

Footwear was not the only labor–management issue. Parking space location, nonalcoholic beer in the lunchroom, and other such issues permeated the plant. Management was concerned about "low morale," and labor was concerned with "lack of respect." After a couple of failed attempts to solve the problem with team building and communication training, management decided to conduct a needs assessment to find out what the real problem was. My firm was asked to do the assessment.

Our assessment process used data collected via Performance Pyramid interviews (protocol available at: NeedsAssessment.missouri.edu), observations, focus groups, and internal reports. This "mixed methods" approach is critical to reaching an understanding of any performance problem. While some conflicting data surfaced, it soon became clear that these variations were consistent with the different perspectives at play. Collectively, the data pointed to one fundamental problem: the power plant was so efficient, so safe, and so modern that many workers were simply bored with their high-paying jobs! How could that be possible? A little background about the workers will help here.

Most of the nonmanagement employees were former Navy, hired due to their extensive experience in nuclear power generation, typically on nuclear-powered submarines. Their expertise was invaluable and too expensive for the power plant to develop. To a man (almost all were males), these highly skilled workers had spent considerable time in high-risk, high-stress situations for extended periods, sometimes submerged for weeks at a time. This background did little to prepare them for employment in a nuclear power plant with eight-hour shifts and a negotiated contract with their superiors.

As one technician commented, "We spend a lot of time acting like snipers, taking pot shots at management just to liven things up." Another lamented, "I wish we would act like we do on those rare occasions when we have a serious problem. We pull together, work as a team, solve the problem, and document what we did." In a nutshell, the work environment was seldom challenging and often boring. One technician noted, "We are kinda' like firefighters, ready to respond to problems, except firefighters get to sleep or play volleyball when there aren't any problems. We have to stay awake, watch gauges, and fill out hourly reports."

Based on the needs assessment findings, we recommended that cross-functional work teams (involving both labor and management) be established and given responsibility for anticipating, preventing, and resolving. The problems ranged from improving foot safety (good-bye flip-flops) to streamlining hourly reporting. One particularly important team focused on "decision-making processes," their goal being to find alternatives to labor–management dispute resolution, often seen as a contentious, if not hostile.

Lessons learned. Three lessons stand out. First, seemingly trivial problems can actually be indicators of larger issues potentially undermining performance. Had our needs assessment focused only on injury reports and OSHA regulations, our recommendations would have not touched the core problem.

Second, the data caused us to broaden our interpretation of "environment" and include "organization culture" in the Pyramid framework. The *intangible* work environment (sniping, petty issues, etc.) was having a significant influence on the prevailing culture (characterized by polarized dispute resolution rather than collective problem solving). Prior to this study, our view of the environment typically focused on tangibles (lighting, temperature, ventilation, etc.). We will continue to expand the Pyramid framework as other performance-impacting factors surface.

NEW DIRECTIONS FOR EVALUATION • DOI: 10.1002/ev

Third, this was our first opportunity to apply the Pyramid in an effort to *prevent* a performance downturn in an organization. The power plant had the highest safety rating in the industry, and it was highly efficient and profitable. To their credit, upper level management sensed the potential for a performance problem to surface and took preventive measures. In this regard, we learned needs assessments and performance improvement efforts can be valuable in organizations NOT experiencing overall performance problem...yet.

Example 2: Too Much to Learn

Ideally, performance improvement efforts are preceded by a comprehensive needs assessment. The needs assessment and the data coming from it establish the base for crafting solutions. This was the case in a large insurance company that was looking for a way to deal with an all-too-common performance problem in the industry. Specifically, it was that reports submitted by less-experienced insurance claim agents usually had many errors (e.g., approving replacement of parts that were not damaged) that resulted in the company paying more than necessary on automotive insurance claims.

From the beginning, the company knew that training was NOT the solution. There were simply too many different makes and models of cars with widely varying mileage and other attributes for someone to learn in a training environment. For example, many auto insurance policies require that the paint on damaged exteriors be returned to the original quality when the car was new. Simple enough, but what about a situation in which one model, for one year, had a quality control problem with one color? A paint job with improved paint might cost more than the original paint, and provide a finish superior to what was required by the policy. Multiply that one bit of automotive trivia by the combinations of makes, models, years, and colors available, and the inadequacy of training becomes readily apparent. The solution: knowledge management. Rather than teach the myriad of details, provide claims agents with ready access to a database where such details are stored.

My firm was asked to help with the early design of the knowledge management system, which was based on an assessment of the overall performance situation. While all the elements in the Pyramid's support system (expectations, tools, rewards, etc.) were in place and aligned with the overall performance goal, it was clear that the training provided by the company was *not* adequate to develop the knowledge required by claims agents. It was also apparent that adequate training would require an inordinate amount of time and money. The remedy was to create a knowledge management system that contained insights typically only found among veteran claims agents.

Was such a large-scale effort worth the time and effort required to build a robust knowledge management solution? The company estimated that if the amount of overpayment on automotive claims were reduced measurably, the company would save approximately $20,000,000 per year! Enough said.

One year later, the company launched a pilot version of the knowledge management system. This was unfolding before the advent of smart phones and high-speed Internet. Indeed, many agents operated out of offices that relied on voice-level phone lines for data communication. As one might expect, the data communication infrastructure was woefully inadequate to support large-scale implementation of a very powerful solution. The light bulb had arrived before the electricity! Coupled with resistance from the corporate Information Technology group, the entire project was put on hold for about two years (at a hidden cost of $40,000,000).

Lessons learned. While the needs assessment accurately produces a powerful solution to the performance problem, the support system—specifically the knowledge management *tools*—was not aligned with the available resources. $20,000,000 annually would be a drop in the bucket compared to the total cost associated with installing a high-speed propri-etary network. Bottom line: we learned the importance of tailoring solutions to the resources that can be brought to the table and the importance of upper level corporate buy-in on performance improvement efforts.

As a footnote, over the last few years we have come to realize that a knowledge management approach that connects people to knowledge may not be as powerful or affordable as a social networking one that ties *knowledgeable people* together. For example, an equipment manufacturing company is likely to have thousands of engineers, mechanics, and assembly workers who collectively make up the manufacturing knowledge base of the company, but it is highly unlikely that any one person has all of the knowledge. A more probable scenario is that while some of the knowledge is held in common, much of it is fragmented across the work force. Capturing, indexing, and making these knowledge fragments accessible is a daunting task, particularly when mechanical changes occur on a regular basis. A more reasoned approach is to build a social network making it possible for manufacturing individuals or groups to find and tap into each other's knowledge. In effect, the "expert system" approach is replaced by an "expertise network."

Example 3: Human Systems Integration Not Integrated

This final example is from a needs assessment conducted by Steege et al. (2012) for the U.S. Army. They used the Performance Pyramid to guide their needs assessment of the Army's human systems integration processes. The project was performed for the Army Research Laboratory's Human Engineering Research and Engineering Directorate. They reported that, prior to the needs assessment, the Directorate had identified the lack of training opportunities as the root of the performance problem, which was characterized as a shortage of human systems integration practitioners with the desired level of expertise. In other words, the Directorate already "knew" that training was the solution.

During their needs assessment, Steege et al. (2012) used the "layered" approach to needs assessment (Wedman, 2010); that is, the needs assessment team worked through successive iterations of data collection, analysis, and decision making, with each additional layer providing greater detail and focus. Data collection methods included examination of documents, interviews, and surveys, using the Pyramid framework to guide the team's work. Not surprisingly, a wide range of needs, including knowledge and skills; tools, environment, and processes; rewards and incentives; expectations and feedback; and organizational vision, were identified. Indeed, most of the elements in the Pyramid framework were impeding optimal performance.

Lessons learned. The Steege et al. article concluded with a discussion of the advantages and disadvantages of the Performance Pyramid. For advantages, the team recognized the Pyramid for its "visual natures" and "straightforward language," attributes the team found as helpful when communicating with clients. The team noted that it provided a structure to guide needs assessment efforts while including a multitude of performance factors at the individual, group, and organizational levels, making for a holistic perspective.

On the disadvantage side, the team learned that the Pyramid may oversimplify the way an organization functions. The Pyramid might not include all the key elements for capturing the root causes of some performance problems and until recently the Pyramid did not include "intangible environment" as an element impacting performance. This insight is consistent with the evolution of the Pyramid. Since its inception, additional elements have been added based on practice, and it is likely more will be incorporated in the future. Practitioners are critical for keeping an eye out for elements that are not included in the Pyramid framework. Still the simple nature of the Pyramid should be maintained.

The team posited the value of the Pyramid could be enhanced by providing (or pointing to) additional tools required to conduct more in-depth examination—task analysis, for example. The same could be said for ways to analyze reward systems, feedback mechanisms, organizational culture, etc. While extremely valuable, I will leave this work for others to undertake and thank Steege et al. for their excellent application of and report about Wedman's Performance Pyramid. Readers interested in greater detail might wish to read their article in the *Performance Improvement* journal.

Selling Needs Assessment and Performance Improvement

It is probably safe to assume that a reader who has reached this point in the chapter has already "bought into" the notion of needs assessment and performance improvement. This assumption seldom plays out in the workplace. Prior to launching a needs assessment project, the team will likely have to "sell" the endeavor to decision makers. Three strategies will help cinch the deal.

First, remember the old adage that "people do not want drills, they want holes." Decision makers are likely to be more interested in the range of potential solutions the needs assessment process will generate than details about how it will be conducted. Phrases like "We might discover that...," "I wonder if...," and "Do you think it's possible that..." can begin to gather support for the project.

Second, it does not matter how important you think the needs assessment process is; it only matters what decision makers think. The change literature is replete with examples of change agents who failed to consider potential adopters' perspectives. If the notion of needs assessment is foreign to decision makers or if they had negative experiences with a previous assessment, their perspectives are all the more important.

Third, manage the selling process by leading decision makers to reach the conclusion that "training" is not likely to be the only solution to a performance problem. A good sales person is going to enable decision makers to reach the conclusion that any number of factors might be impeding performance, including but not limited to performers' lack of knowledge and skills. This last point was critical in my efforts to secure a large corporation's vice president for human resources endorsement to change the corporation's training division to a performance improvement division. I had 15 minutes to "make the sale"; he bought it in 10, and spent an additional 20 minutes talking about how to move forward!

Linking Needs Assessment and Evaluation

As mentioned earlier, HPT is the process of identifying performance needs, implementing solutions to meet these needs, and evaluating the impact of the solutions on performance and the resulting outcomes. It might be helpful to think of needs assessment and evaluation as bookends, supporting implementation (Figure 4.3).

Extending the bookend analogy, one bookend is seldom an adequate support, but collectively they perform the support function quite well. Implementing solutions without a needs assessment is akin to using a "spray and pray" strategy (spray the performance problem with a wide range of solutions and hope some hit the target). Implementing solutions without a follow-up evaluation immediately raises the question, "Did the solutions produce the desired outcomes?" When implementation is preceded by a needs assessment and followed with evaluation, the focus of implementation is sharpened and outcomes are documented and in turn evaluation findings often form the basis for additional, highly targeted, needs assessments, resulting in a complete system.

NEW DIRECTIONS FOR EVALUATION • DOI: 10.1002/ev

Figure 4.3. Linking Needs Assessment and Evaluation

Conclusion

This chapter has provided a brief overview of Wedman's Performance Pyramid—a systemic framework for needs assessment and performance improvement. Three examples were used to illustrate how the Pyramid can be applied in business and military settings. Strategies for "selling" needs assessment and performance improvement were provided, along with a simple description of the link between needs assessment and evaluation.

An essential feature of the Pyramid is the notion of adequacy and alignment. Vision, resources, and support system elements must be sufficient to accomplish the desired outcomes (adequacy), and work in concert (alignment). While continuous monitoring and change management were in the model (see Figure 4.2), the importance of these processes was not addressed. Both warrant elaboration and documentation in the professional and applied literature.

References

Gayeski, D. M. (1999). Frontiers for human performance technology in contemporary organizations. In H. Stolovitch & E. Keeps (Eds.), *Handbook of human performance technology* (2nd ed., pp. 936–949). San Francisco, CA: Jossey-Bass.

Gilbert, T. (1978). *Human competence: Engineering worthy performance.* New York, NY: McGraw-Hill.

Harless, J. H. (1973). An analysis of front-end analysis. *Improving Human Performance: A Research Quarterly, 4,* 229–244.

Mager, R., & Pipe, P. (1970). *Analyzing performance problems* (2nd ed.). Belmont, CA: Pitman Learning.

Rossett, A., & Czech, C. (1995). They really wanna, but... the aftermath of professional preparation in performance technology. *Performance Improvement Quarterly, 8*(4), 115–132.

Steege, L. B., Marra, R. M., & Jones, K. (2012). Meeting needs assessment challenges: Applying the performance pyramid in the U.S. Army. *Performance Improvement*, *51*(10), 31–41.

Wedman, J. (2010). The performance pyramid. In R. Watkins & D. Leigh (Eds.), *Handbook of improving performance in the workplace, Vol. 2, The handbook of selecting and implementing performance interventions* (pp. 51–74). San Francisco, CA: Wiley.

JOHN WEDMAN (1949–2013) *was a professor emeritus of information science and learning technologies at the University of Missouri at Columbia.*

NEW DIRECTIONS FOR EVALUATION • DOI: 10.1002/ev

Lepicki, T., & Boggs, A. (2014). Needs assessments to determine training requirements. In
J. W. Altschuld & R. Watkins (Eds.), *Needs assessment: Trends and a view toward the future.*
New Directions for Evaluation, 144, 61–74.

5

Needs Assessments to Determine Training Requirements

Traci Lepicki, Adrienne Boggs

Abstract

This chapter gives the reader a close look at what a workforce development needs assessment might entail, as well as the twists and turns that are inevitably encountered in almost any assessment of this type. The authors describe a case example in the context of direct service providers (home healthcare personnel, nursing assistants, and so forth) and a complex needs assessment project in this area that employed a three-phase model of needs assessment. They note that the phases, which seem distinct on paper, blur and overlap in practice so that rigid adherence to them must be tempered by what the real world imposes on the situation. In the last part of the chapter the role and stance of those collecting and analyzing needs data are examined, as well as lessons learned from having to make various adjustments to the assessment process as it moves forward. © Wiley Periodicals, Inc., and the American Evaluation Association.

Orchestrating an Assessment

Are needs assessment and training needs assessment the same? Are they in harmony or disconnected? In the assessment literature there is a cacophony of terms; multiple descriptions, models, and processes are offered, many times used interchangeably (Rossett, 1987; Triner, Greenberry, Watkins, 1996; Watkins, Leigh, Platt, & Kaufman, 1998). Certainly, our jobs as assessors would be easier if the definitions were in concert; however, the literature features different voices, concepts, and practices. The goal of this chapter is to position a specific workforce development and training endeavor within the ensemble, adding to the overall assessment symphony.

Needs assessment blurs the line between the public and private sectors when we start to examine the relationships between the worlds of work, education, and public policy. As the marketplace changes, occupations are created or phased out, revealing multiple needs; not the least of which are related to "retooling" education systems and retraining incumbent workers (Carnevale, Smith, & Strohl, 2010). For instance, with the greening of the economy in California, a workforce education and training needs assessment was conducted that elicited needs related to the nature of green jobs and the economy, the basics of labor supply and demand, and an array of education and training programs (Zabin et al., 2011). It resulted in a lengthy report with implications and recommendations targeting a full spectrum of stakeholders, from public-sector education to private-sector training. This example suggests that conducting an assessment can uncover layers of needs with related causes and a multitude of possible solutions— often obscuring the boundaries of needs assessment and training needs assessment.

Assessment at Work in Ohio

Multiple needs and multiple solutions equally apply to our work. In the Ohio project, *Ohio Direct Service Workforce Initiative*, we investigated conditions related to direct care workers—*home health aides, personal aides, nursing assistants*, and others who provide "frontline" support to clients in home and community settings. As a workforce development strategy for the state, the initiative was focused on creating a career lattice—a framework that arrays competencies across sectors and settings to delineate career and educational progression (O*NET Resource Center, n.d.). The desired results of the lattice for the worker, employer, and agency stakeholders are in Table 5.1. The underlying proposition was that by creating a compelling structure with pathways to training, credentialing, and job opportunities, the status of the direct care profession would be elevated, thus attracting and retaining a quality workforce in order to meet growing demand.

At the onset, we understood there was a desired solution within the education and training context. However, all too often clients tend to focus on solutions first before digging deeper into the problem, the actual need (i.e., the underlying conditions that contribute to the situation). Following Rossett (1987), the client may have a sense about needs through individual opinions or ideas. Or the client may be confounded by training as a part of training needs assessment as Triner et al. (1996) offer, "Why go through

Table 5.1. Aims of Ohio Direct Service Workforce Initiative Career Lattice

For the worker, the lattice will:
- Increase quality and consistency of training based on common competencies
- Increase flexibility, providing lateral movement between sectors
- Connect all direct care workers to career pathways
- Provide opportunities to advance to other professional positions

For the employer, the lattice will:
- Reduce cost by reducing the need to retrain workers at every job change
- Provide a means to determine whether the workforce is competent
- Reduce turnover when workers feel competent to perform their jobs
- Provide for recruitment of workers from diverse backgrounds into positions where diversity is lacking

For government agencies, the lattice will:
- Unify systems that are often in silos
- Support state efforts to develop a consolidated waiver program by providing a more uniformly trained workforce
- Provide a means for funders to determine whether the workforce is competent

Note. Adapted and modified from Crane-Ross, 2012, *Health and Human Services Lattice.* Columbus: Ohio Colleges of Medicine Government Resource Center, The Ohio State University.

the process of needs assessment if the decision as to a solution—training—has already been made?" (pp. 52–53). With this project we knew it was important to step back and ensure that the effort did not jump to solution strategies prematurely without fully examining needs (Altschuld & Kumar, 2010).

Getting Started

Drawing from Altschuld and Witkin's (2000) three-phase model, our efforts with the *Ohio Direct Service Workforce Initiative* began in 2010 with determining what we already knew about the current conditions as well as implications from healthcare models and educational trends. Table 5.2 offers an overview of key project activities aligned to the model. Starting first with a leadership team comprised of researchers and the sponsoring agency, a broad consortium of stakeholders (consumers, workers, employers, associations) was convened to guide the effort, a Needs Assessment Committee or NAC (Witkin, 1984). This group informed the assessment design, assisted in the recruitment of individuals throughout the project, and aided in interpretation/reaction to data gathered and summarized.

An early consideration was the level of needs as determined by the roles of stakeholders. In accord with Altschuld and Lepicki (2009), Table 5.3 contains the primary levels of need, arrayed from consumer to employer. Later in this chapter as the conversation shifts to training needs, the levels also shift.

Table 5.2. Activities Aligned to Needs Assessment Phases

Phases	Key Project Activities	Purpose
I. Preassessment (initiating the project, reviewing existing data, determining how to proceed)	NAC formation	Guide project and assist with specific activities (e.g., recruitment, data interpretation, policy recommendations)
	Literature review	Understand context and needs in general across levels
II. Assessment (gathering/analyzing data, determining discrepancies/causes, proposing priorities/solutions)	Employer interviews	Determine employer-level needs to inform additional data collection and analysis
	Research projects	Gather more data and provide causal analysis for identified needs across levels
	Job task analysis	Determine job tasks at the worker level, identify job task discrepancies across occupational areas, and prioritize competency development activities
	Competency correlations	Identify discrepancies between proposed and currently required competencies and recommend solution strategies to resolve them
III. Postassessment[a] (implementing solutions/plans, evaluating the assessment)	Competency, test, and curriculum development	Implement prioritized solution strategies focused on education and training

[a]Since the Ohio Direct Service Workforce Initiative is an ongoing project, further solution strategies, action plans, and evaluation processes may be carried out expanding the activities of the postassessment phase.

Table 5.3. Levels of Need

Level	Level Description	Level Example
1	"End users," recipients of goods and services	Consumers of health and human services
2	Providers of goods and services	Direct care workers
3	System/organization in which providers reside	Employers of direct care workers

Gaps in Health and Human Services

From a quick review of the literature and initial NAC conversations, it was apparent that there are significant challenges to attracting and retaining highly qualified direct care workers (current conditions). The work is considered low-wage with a high rate of turnover. There are no clear career

Table 5.4. Sampling of Direct Service Workforce Needs

Area	Current State	Desired State
Supply and demand	Workers in demand Inadequate supply of workers	Supply of workers commensurate with demand
Employment "churn"	High worker turnover	Reduced turnover Workers retained
Wages and benefits	Low-wage Little to no benefits	Improved wage Increased benefits
Education and training	Lack of education and training	Increased opportunities Standardized education and training

paths and limited opportunities for education beyond only short-term on-the-job training for specifics tasks and needs (Institute of Medicine, 2008). This is true in other countries as well; the United Kingdom, Ireland, and Canada are experiencing similar challenges with direct care (Spencer, Martin, Bourgeault, & O'Shea, 2010).

At the same time, in terms of the future of the direct care workforce, there is a national trend for increasing attention being given to the area. The United States is facing a demand problem based on the size of the baby boom generation and increased longevity. According to Cauley (2011), the population over 60 will double within the next twenty years, and those most likely to need long-term care, adults over 85, will increase five times. The patterns here and internationally reflect the need and will even generalize to transitional and developing economies (Fujisawa & Colombo, 2009; Organization for Economic Cooperation and Development, 2011).

When we started the project, discrepancies between the quality and the quantity of the workforce were well documented (Table 5.4). The situation was obvious—the need for the direct care providers is expected to increase dramatically coupled with a lack of attractiveness of the profession.

Addressing the Nontraining Needs

In 2011 Phase II, the actual assessment began (Altschuld & Witkin, 2000). Informed by policymakers and preassessment (Phase I) findings, the endeavor required digging deeper into the four need areas in Table 5.4. A number of them have impacts on employers (Level 3), and their engagement is a key component of efforts dealing with workforce development (U.S. Department of Education, Office of Vocational and Adult Education, 2012). To garner buy-in and to gather more data, the chief executive officers and human resources directors of service providers were interviewed. First, they were presented with the career lattice followed by asking them to react to it and offer advantages, disadvantages, benefits, and hesitations resulting from their understanding of the lattice coupled with their experiences as business leaders. Comments were organized into five themes: cost efficiency, innovations, worker recruitment and retention, regulations related to funding and reimbursement, and education and training resources. Only the latter theme tied to the education and training need area.

Because the themes extended beyond education and training, we understood that a solution strategy focused on education and training would not necessarily have an instrumental effect on the other need areas; more work was to be done. Given that the needs were not isolated, attention broadened to investigation of supply and demand, employment "churn," and wages and benefits. With the potential for multiple competing needs, we turned to Kaufman's (1998) description of needs assessment in which he posited that the prioritization of needs be based on the cost to meet each need (closing a gap) versus the cost for ignoring it (not closing a gap). This then led to a host of new questions and considerations, including for example:

- What is the compensation or value of work costs to employees for what is considered "dirty work" (Stacey, 2005)?
- What are the quality-of-care costs to consumers?
- What are the time and financial implications for employers?

In 2012, Larsen noted that the costs per hire ranged from $3,000 to $6,000 and that supervisors invest 18% of their time to employees because turnover approaches 50%; thus, there are recruitment and retention issues with associated monetary issues. At this stage in the project, research (causes of turnover, further examination of care settings, identification of best practices in care integration) was undertaken by other investigators to better understand these nontraining concerns. Multiple methods were employed, including mining existing employment and healthcare data systems, conducting facility site visits, and interviewing employers and workers. These nontraining need investigations resulted in reimbursement and funding recommendations for policymakers, as well as business management recommendations for employers in areas such as hiring practices, client to worker ratios, and incentivizing performance.

Analysis Leading to Competencies

Returning to education and training, broadly speaking we saw a range of needs related to direct care but did not specifically know about the occupations that provide the care. Based on Gupta, Sleezer, and Russ-Eft (2007), attention was turned to analyzing the occupations that comprise the direct care worker area using the DACUM technique (Developing A Curriculum; Norton & Moser, 2008). It was chosen because it balances process and costs for implementation. It includes the following:

Figure 5.1. Job Task Analysis Sequence

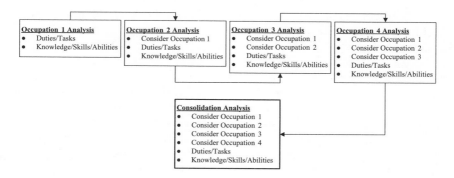

1. Recruiting a small sample of expert workers of varying demographics (e.g., rural/urban location, large/small agency size) to participate in a two-day analysis panel.
2. Facilitating the panel in the development of duty and task statements describing an occupation.
3. Assisting the panel in listing of knowledge and skills associated with the occupation.
4. Capturing lists of behaviors, characteristics, tools, equipment, and future trends for the occupation.
5. Formatting and processing a draft occupational chart based on panel consensus.
6. Verifying the chart by surveying a larger sample of workers and other stakeholders.

For our part of the project, job incumbents (expert workers in direct care) via a series of two-day panels described what they do through brainstorming and storyboarding techniques designed to encourage discussion and consensus building. Home health direct care workers began the DACUM process, and subsequent panels in behavioral health, nursing facilities, and developmental disabilities completed it, each being informed by the previous panels' analyses (Figure 5.1). This led to the duties, tasks, knowledge areas, and skills for each respective occupation area, which were subsequently verified through determining task criticality (measurement of task importance and frequency of its performance).

A fifth panel was convened to analyze the findings from the four previous ones to establish commonalities and differences. The expectation, informed by the NAC, was that there would be fewer differences (a desired state of little to no discrepancy) between the DACUM charts, indicating a core set of tasks, knowledge areas, and skills. This consolidation process resulted in a total of 36 tasks across the four occupations (home health, nursing facilities, behavioral health, developmental disabilities), and 61 tasks were common to home health, nursing facilities, and developmental disabilities. Thirty-six knowledge areas and 37 skills fit all four occupations, and 56 knowledge areas and 39 skills were seen for home health, nursing facilities, and developmental disabilities.

Beginning with McClelland (1973) and extending into the present, assessing performance based on competence is a tenet of human resource management. For Ennis (2008), "a competency is the capability of applying or using knowledge, skills, abilities, behaviors, and personal characteristics to successfully perform critical work tasks, specific functions, or operate in a given role or position" (pp. 4–5). From that perspective and the outcomes of the consolidation panel, policymakers prioritized the core competencies for the direct care workforce as the tasks, knowledge areas, and skills common to home health, nursing facilities, and developmental disabilities. The Phase III (postassessment) strategy was to move forward with tests and curriculum development aligned to the core competencies.

Competencies Leading to Additional Analysis

In the spring of 2012, we moved into specific postassessment work focused on examining tasks in more detail to provide materials for testing. Heterogeneous teams of direct care workers across the four occupations who had participated in the DACUM panels examined the 61 core tasks relative to the steps in them and the tools, equipment, supplies, and materials; key knowledge and skill; safety concerns; worker behaviors; frequent errors; and criteria for successful performance of each step. Later, writers used the task analysis results to derive plausible test items. At the same time, we conducted more Phase II needs assessment efforts—identifying discrepancies between competency sets to inform curriculum development. We reviewed the newly developed core competencies in terms of existing competencies and training regulations to determine gaps in content and requirements. This was also input for developing new curriculum mapped to the core competencies.

Shifting Perspectives on Training

Although we have largely focused on identifying competencies, they are only one part of the training picture. Besides content based on competencies, Surface (2013) suggests that equal attention should be paid to *who* needs to be trained. When we began to give greater attention to what the direct care worker needs to know and be able to do (competency development), this centered around Level 2—the worker. But, from a training perspective, that is a slight shift in the levels of need (Altschuld & Lepicki, 2009) with Level 2 in effect becoming a pseudo Level 1 group. The worker moves from being the provider of service (Level 2) to the recipient of service as "end users" of training (Level 1). Educators and trainers become Level 2 providers, and the systems in which education and training programs exist become Level 3.

Within the project, by adjusting the need levels, we are pushed to re-examine and reassess needs. Surface (2013) further notes the importance of *how* to conduct training and that training needs assessment informs instructional design. Crucial questions here might be:

1. What training programs currently exist?
2. To what content are current training programs aligned?
3. Do training programs already cover the competencies? To what degree?
4. What adjustments have to be made in content and instructional delivery to address the new competencies or enhance older ones?
5. Is there a willingness to revise existing programs?
6. Will the demand for training offset investment in redesigning training programs?
7. Should new training programs be created?

A multitude of decision making is necessary to adjust or develop training, whether from new competencies or other influences. Lastly, Surface (2013) asserts that workplace trends (shifting demographics, globalization) and learning ones (informal learning, technology-delivered instruction) factor into training needs.

Implications for Workforce Development

There are a number of aspects of the current project that may be applicable to other workforce development projects. In the healthcare field alone, there is much opportunity to be gained from what was done in the *Ohio Direct Service Workforce Initiative*. There is growing momentum for continuing to examine needs related to competency development as in mental health with new occupations such as *peer support professional, recovery coach*, and *healthcare navigator*. Education and training systems built on competencies and career pathways will be of interest in workforce development as occupational fields evolve to keep pace with industry demands within a changing knowledge and service economy.

In addition to competencies (what is learned) and career pathways (how learning is structured), advances in technology continue to challenge our thinking about what learning prepares us to do (work)—what it is and where it happens. We are pushed to reconsider how work is carried out (redefining the role of the worker) and how workers interact (mobile technology, social media) in a real-time (instant messaging) marketplace. Certainly, this affects how we design and deliver training and move forward with robust educational systems and advancement opportunities for professionalizing the relevant workforce.

NEW DIRECTIONS FOR EVALUATION • DOI: 10.1002/ev

Assessment Lessons and Considerations

In many respects, the work of the *Ohio Direct Service Workforce Initiative* resulted in more questions for us as investigators than answers. Through years of activity associated with the project, we have reflected on our informal learning along the way and appreciate the nuances of needs assessment and training needs assessment.

The Assessment Process

Is this a linear process? It may be somewhat sequential, but in our experience it was not a "one and done" activity; the assessment endeavor was sometimes iterative. Information gathered throughout the project was brought back to the NAC (Phase I) for constant guidance and interpretation, continuing to cycle back to the first phase. Literature review (Phase I) did inform the Phase II activities (employer interviews, research projects, job task analysis, and competency correlations); however, the four Phase II activities did not necessarily flow one to the next. Instead, they were somewhat distinct and provided a composite of discrepancies, causes, and possible solutions. Analogously, as Phase III activities are completed (competency, test, and curriculum development), more assessment may be inevitable such as determining specific needs associated with revising or creating training programs.

The Assessment Levels

Did we address all the levels affected by the *Ohio Direct Service Workforce Initiative*? In 2005, Kaufman explained mega thinking connected to his Organizational Elements Model by relating planning levels (Mega, Macro, Micro, Process, Input) with organizational elements (outcome, outputs, products, processes, inputs). Questions à la Kaufman might be:

- With the current project did we devote enough attention to the mega level and the well-being of society at large?
- How does the project connect to increased healthcare outcomes in the United States?
- Could it result in a higher standard of living for a whole segment of workers in direct care?
- Have we pushed far enough with professionalizing the field?

Early in the project, the desired results of a career lattice were offered (Table 5.1); in our data collection we focused largely on the worker, employer, and agency stakeholders (Table 5.3). But where were the consumers of health and human services in the assessment?

Altschuld and Kumar (2010) noted that Level 1 (consumers) may be overlooked because many times assessments are driven by Level 2 (providers). If we reconsider the concept of mega thinking and give equal attention to all levels of stakeholders, we could have a richer picture of the initiative. By including society as a collection of consumers in the mix, additional benefits such as the following could arise:

- Increased client access to services.
- Expanded consumer choice and empowerment.
- Reduced client cost (home and community care is less expensive than acute care and long-term facility care).

We assume there could be others had we done more to include the societal voice, more embedding of consumer views in the research projects and consumers on the NAC. Could the needs assessments have been enriched by the mega level with a greater focus on the Level 1 end user?

While this may have led to a deeper, more meaningful set of results, there is a price to pay to achieve it. The project timeline would have to be extended, and sponsors are anxious to get results more quickly. Budgets for the assessment would have to be higher and include more resources for maintaining communication and involvement. We secured buy-in from workers, employers, and agency stakeholders because in one way or another, this initiative connects to their work, but for consumers this is not the case. The assessment staff would need an abundance of skills to work across constituent groups with particular attention paid to engaging consumers. The team would require a broader array of specialized expertise and experiences to encompass a substantially enlarged scope of work.

The Assessor and the Sponsor

What is the relationship between the assessor and the project sponsor? It is important to develop an early and strong rapport with the sponsoring agency. As was the case for us, at the beginning of the project, the assessor is likely an unknown quantity. Having a sponsor who is a champion can head off skepticism, if it exists, build the assessor's credibility with stakeholders, and facilitate communication and data collection.

The Assessor and Postassessment

What is the responsibility of the needs assessor in postassessment (Phase III)? As Ohio continues with development, current direct care workers and those considering the area will need guidance on career choices. Once the testing system is in place, care must be taken to ensure that it is field-tested and that components operate as planned, and maintained and updated as necessary.

Similarly, across educational systems competencies should be revisited on a regular basis to ensure quality and relevance; curriculum alignments will need to be reviewed. Over time how do we plan for needs associated with the maintenance and upgrading that will come to the fore (Altschuld & Kumar, 2010)? Ongoing conversations with state agencies responsible for technical education will be essential.

But, the question becomes is it our job as needs assessors to facilitate those conversations, keeping pace with the evolving career and training demands of direct care work in Ohio? It is likely not the assessor role, but there are advantages to switching roles if possible to add value in the postassessment. In our case we are moving from assessors to developers, implementing solution strategies and action plans for competency, test and curriculum development. There are numerous advantages to being a part of postassessment, including:

- We know the big picture and context to apply to our new role.
- We have established working relationships and credibility with the stakeholders.
- We are invested in the success of the entire initiative.

Likewise, we can leverage the project to showcase other staff expertise and extend our funding. Of course, there are added costs with added work; however, there are cost savings resulting from already being strategically aligned with the sponsor, eliminating the "start-up curve" that typically comes at the beginning of a brand new project.

Assessment in Harmony

We suspect that many assessments in complicated systems encounter complex problems, many opinions. Our project was no different and problems involving training and nontraining issues will generally not have simple (or singular) solutions. Because of this, we attempted to gain as much clarity as possible on the situation and the need for the assessment, upfront in the project. We then continued to test our assumptions, gain clarity throughout the effort, and draw from needs assessment and training needs assessment approaches.

Is a blended approach useful? At the beginning of the project, the assumption was that a training needs assessment was in order, and we proceeded to investigate needs where training was the probable solution using employer interview and job task analysis (DACUM) processes. However, aspects of the project unrelated to training called for different strategies. For instance, the Phase II research projects with their focus on turnover, care settings, and care integration necessitated their own processes and when they are completed may likely result in another set of priorities and recommended solution strategies apart from the job task analysis and competency investigation.

Throughout the project we shifted in and out of assessment phases, reconfigured our thinking of need levels, and oscillated between needs assessment and training needs assessment. Building from needs assessment approaches (Kaufman, 1998; Witkin, 1984) provided a useful framework for training needs assessment approaches; combining the two was utilitarian.

Although an assessment process is guided by a model or framework, it must be approached openly with anticipation of adjustments along the way. Assessors must be prepared to adapt or change course at times always within the larger schema of what the overall context entails. Flexibility is necessary as rigid adherence to one model almost always will not work. There is no "one size fits all" approach. Customizing from the multiple descriptions, models, and processes is key to orchestrating a successful assessment. We must continually adapt and blend our practices as the context changes— always with an eye toward evaluating our efforts and improving methods.

References

Altschuld, J. W., & Kumar, D. D. (2010). *Needs assessment: An overview* (Vol. 1). Thousand Oaks, CA: Sage.

Altschuld, J. W., & Lepicki, T. (2009). Needs assessment in human performance interventions. In R. Watkins & D. Leigh (Eds.), *Handbook of improving performance in the workplace, Vol. 2, The handbook of selecting and implementing performance interventions* (pp. 771–791). San Francisco, CA: Wiley.

Altschuld, J. W., & Witkin, B. R. (2000). *From needs assessment to action: Transforming needs into solution strategies*. Thousand Oaks, CA: Sage.

Carnevale, A., Smith, N., & Strohl, J. (2010). *Help wanted: Projections of jobs and education requirements through 2018*. Retrieved from https://georgetown.app.box.com /s/ursjbxaym2np1v8mgrv7

Cauley, K. (2011). *Identifying competencies of Ohio's long term care workers serving the elderly population in Ohio*. Dayton, OH: Boonshoft School of Medicine and School of Professional Psychology, Wright State University.

Crane-Ross, D. (2012). *Health and human service lattice*. Columbus: Ohio Colleges of Medicine Government Resource Center, The Ohio State University.

Ennis, M. (2008). *Competency models: A review of the literature and the role of the employment and training administration (ETA)*. Department of Labor, Office of Policy Development and Research. Retrieved from http://wdr.doleta.gov/research/FullText _Documents/Competency%20Models%20-%20A%20Review%20of%20Literature %20and%20the%20Role%20of%20the%20Employment%20and%20Training %2Administration.pdf

Fujisawa, R., & Colombo, F. (2009). *The long-term care workforce: Overview and strategies to adapt supply to a growing demand*. Paris, France: Organization for Economic Cooperation and Development.

Gupta, K., Sleezer, C. M., & Russ-Eft, D. F. (2007). *A practical guide to needs assessment* (2nd ed.). San Francisco, CA: Wiley.

Institute of Medicine. (2008). *Retooling for an aging America: Building the health care workforce*. Retrieved from http://www.iom.edu/Reports/2008/Retooling-for-an-Aging-America-Building-the-Health-Care-Workforce.aspx

Kaufman, R. (1998). *Strategic thinking: A guide to identifying and solving problems* (Rev. ed.). Arlington, VA: American Society for Training & Development.

Kaufman, R. (2005). Defining and delivering measurable value: A mega thinking and planning primer. *Performance Improvement Quarterly, 18*(3), 6–16.

Larsen, S. (2012, October). *State efforts to enhance the quality of direct service workers*. Presented at the Ohio's Direct Service Workforce Applied Research Conference, Columbus, OH.

McClelland, D. C. (1973). Testing for competence rather than for intelligence. *American Psychologist, 28*(1), 1–14.

Norton, R. W., & Moser, J. (2008). *The DACUM handbook*. Columbus: Center on Education and Training for Employment, The Ohio State University.

O*NET Resource Center. (n.d.). *Career ladders and lattices*. Retrieved from http://www.onetcenter.org/ladders.html

Organization for Economic Cooperation and Development. (2011). *Help wanted: Providing and paying for long-term care*. Paris, France: Author.

Rossett, A. (1987). *Training needs assessment*. Englewood Cliffs, NJ: Educational Technology.

Spencer, S., Martin, S., Bourgeault, I. V., & O'Shea, E. (2010). *The role of migrant care workers in ageing societies: Report on research findings in the United Kingdom, Ireland, Canada and the United States*. Geneva, Switzerland: International Organization for Migration. Retrieved from http://publications.iom.int/bookstore/free/MRS41.pdf

Stacey, C. L. (2005). Finding dignity in dirty work: The constraints and rewards of low-wage home care labour. *Sociology of Health & Illness, 27*(6), 831–854.

Surface, E. A. (2013). Training needs assessment: Aligning learning and capability with performance requirements and organizational objectives. In M. A. Wilson, W. Bennett, S. Gibson, & G. Allinger (Eds.), *Handbook of work analysis: Methods, systems, application, and science of work measurement in organizations* (pp. 438–468). New York, NY: Routledge Academic.

Triner, D., Greenberry, A., & Watkins, R. (1996). Training needs assessment: A contradiction in terms? *Educational Technology, 36*(6), 51–55.

U.S. Department of Education, Office of Vocational and Adult Education. (2012). *Integrating industry-driven competencies in education and training through employer engagement: Community college virtual symposium*. Retrieved from http://www2.ed.gov/about/offices/list/ovae/pi/cclo/brief-4-employer-engagement.pdf

Watkins, R., Leigh, D., Platt, W., & Kaufman, R. (1998). Needs assessment: A digest, review, and comparison of needs assessment literature. *Performance Improvement Journal, 37*(7), 40–53.

Witkin, B. R. (1984). *Assessing needs in educational and social programs: Using information to make decisions, set priorities, and allocate resources*. San Francisco, CA: Jossey-Bass.

Zabin, C., Chapple, K., Avis, E., Halpern-Finnerty, J., Lester, T. W., Freely, J., ... Church, Z. (2011). *California workforce education and training needs assessment for energy efficiency, distributed generation, and demand response*. Berkley, CA: Donald Vial Center on Employment in the Green Economy, University of California. Retrieved from http://www.irle.berkeley.edu/vial/publications/ca_workforce_needs_assessment.html

Traci Lepicki is the associate director of CETE in the College of Education and Human Ecology, The Ohio State University.

Adrienne Boggs is a program manager at CETE in the College of Education and Human Ecology, The Ohio State University.

New Directions for Evaluation • DOI: 10.1002/ev

Meiers, M. W., Watkins, R., & Song, K. M. (2014). International perspectives: Similarities and differences around the globe. In J. W. Altschuld & R. Watkins (Eds.), *Needs assessment: Trends and a view toward the future. New Directions for Evaluation, 144*, 75–87.

6

International Perspectives: Similarities and Differences Around the Globe

Maurya West Meiers, Ryan Watkins, Kristin Marsh Song

Abstract

Needs are not uniquely American. From Johannesburg and Helsinki to Cairo and Santiago, they are assessed around the world in a variety of contexts and conditions. Needs assessments often cross borders and cultural boundaries, attempting to systematically assist communities, organizations, and people in making better informed decisions. This complexity can improve the results of an assessment, while at the same time presenting the assessor and the methods used with many practical challenges. In response, the focus of this chapter has to do with successfully conducting needs assessments in diverse international contexts. Offering practical tips, the foundation of the chapter provides real-world guidance for handling many of the obstacles faced in needs assessments. © Wiley Periodicals, Inc., and the American Evaluation Association.

Introduction

Through experience conducting needs assessments in varied countries around the globe, the authors have gained a deep understanding of the theoretical underpinnings and practical realities of international needs assessment work. An examination of the contrasts and similarities in needs assessment practices from Rwanda to Laos to Germany, and the accommodations that have to be made for various contexts, provides useful guidance for all who do needs assessment work, including those involved

New Directions for Evaluation, no. 144, Winter 2014 © 2014 Wiley Periodicals, Inc., and the American Evaluation Association. Published online in Wiley Online Library (wileyonlinelibrary.com) • DOI: 10.1002/ev.20104 much closer to home. In this chapter, we first explore when and how needs assessments are used to guide decisions in international contexts. Then we extrapolate lessons learned that can improve your professional practice no matter where you live or work.

Why Needs Assessment?

When is the last time you came across the head of a government agency or nonprofit who complained of having *just too much money?* Never, right? Municipalities, schools, nongovernmental organizations (NGOs), national governments, private-sector companies, and other groups all have at least one thing in common: a shortage of resources to meet the desired wants and needs of their respective citizens and stakeholders. It's not only the total amount of money that is available that is important, but also how we use it and the other resources that we have. Failing to plan for achieving desired results is essentially planning to fail at achieving them.

When they are simple or routine, we may be able to get away with less rigorous planning and needs assessment. But when projects are more complex (such as in international contexts), planning becomes exponentially more important. In such instances, there are often diverse and divergent interests among stakeholders, existing inequities, socioeconomic and political obstacles, inconsistent governance, a lack of physical and policy infrastructure, and many other challenges. Planning, and more specifically needs assessments as part of the planning, is therefore crucial to making informed decisions about what is to be accomplished and weighing alternatives for getting those results.

Planning is not, of course, a complete panacea in making projects successful. It will not build roads, bridges, schools, or dams, but it can help us avoid failures, minimize risks, and, ideally, lead to desired results.

From large-scale needs assessments, such as those associated with the Millennium Development Goals (United Nations Millennium Project, 2004), to smaller ones done by local nonprofits or for-profit organizations, processes for identifying and prioritizing needs are often used to guide decisions. Given this essential role in informing decisions, needs assessments offer diverse opportunities for professionals with the appropriate skills to have substantial impact and to prepare subsequent efforts for ongoing monitoring and evaluation. After all, many parallel tools and techniques are applied across both needs assessments and evaluations, though at different times and with distinctive goals. Needs assessments, for instance, frequently sit in the coveted "front end" of project design, and especially in international development projects, they can serve as a catalyst for positive outcomes and impacts.

International perspectives on needs and needs assessment are, by definition, diverse. From Kenya to Lithuania to Honduras, the role they play

New Directions for Evaluation • DOI: 10.1002/ev

Figure 6.1. Needs

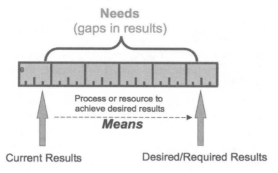

Source: Based on Kaufman (2011).

in decisions ranges from nonexistent to very systematic. In some regions, the use of a needs assessment may be an automatic assumption, whereas in others it may be almost unheard of, and some regions may be doing very similar activities using different words to describe it. The economic development of a country also shapes the context in which assessments are carried out—in developing economies, politics and funding often mean that needs assessments focus heavily on public-sector efficiency and performance, rather than private-sector enterprise.

Given this diversity and our experiences, we will draw primarily from the international development context. This does not cover the entire spectrum of international needs assessments (private sector ones, those in developed economies, etc.). Nevertheless, the lessons here provide a starting place for ongoing dialogues around the challenges and opportunities of conducting assessments in complex international settings.

Are We on the Same Page?

To verify that we have a common understanding of what we are referring to as "needs assessments," let's start with a basic definition of needs. Since the 1970s, Roger Kaufman has offered a definition of "needs" as *gaps in results* (see Watkins & Kavale, Chapter 2 of this issue for further discussion on defining needs). From a performance perspective, this definition is useful for assessing needs as gaps between *What Should Be* results and *What Is* results (or Need = What Should Be – What Is). The size and importance of gaps can then be compared and contrasted to inform decisions (see Figure 6.1).

NEW DIRECTIONS FOR EVALUATION • DOI: 10.1002/ev

Applying this definition of needs, in needs assessment, we identify and prioritize needs in order to guide decisions. As an example, a country's need associated with childhood malaria could be defined by the target number of infections minus the current number of infections. Needs associated with HIV/AIDS, poverty, gender-based violence, and other issues can likewise be assessed in comparison to malaria, focusing on gaps in results and the costs to close or not close them in order to inform decisions (Kaufman & Guerra-Lopez, 2013).

As you can see, the scope of needs assessments can range from light to exhaustive. Regardless of scope, there are however some basic steps to follow when conducting an assessment—and these are presented elsewhere (e.g., Altschuld, 2010; Kaufman & Guerra-Lopez, 2013; Watkins, West Meiers, & Visser, 2012). They focus your work on informing decisions about what to do next. To achieve this, we turn our attention to several everyday questions that you'll want to have answered in order to get the most out of your needs assessment. These include:

- *What are our needs?* In other words, what is the gap between our current versus desired results? We answer this by defining what results should be achieved and then analyzing current performance in comparison.
- *What are the causes of the needs?* Understanding the *root causes* is essential, since quality decisions about what to do must be informed by accurate understanding of the needs and their causes. This will eventually lead us to look at possible solutions.
  For example, what might be at the heart of less-than-adequate teacher performance in a district? To investigate root causes we might ask about standards for recruitment (such as a certain type of teaching certification, test score, etc.). Or we might examine data to see if the wrong people are being selected for jobs. Likewise, we may collect information to determine if only poorly qualified individuals apply for positions, and if new teacher supervision is adequate for the first three years of employment. From an incentive perspective, we might also look at the alignment of what we are assessing to measure performance and incentives associated with those behaviors. Similarly, causal factors could be explored from a variety of viewpoints in order to determine why the identified and measured needs exist.
- *What are the most important needs to address?* Often we enter a decision believing (or assuming) that a certain need is an obvious priority. Sometimes a needs assessment will confirm this, but more typically we learn that the complexity of the challenges and opportunities associated with the decision make defining priorities more difficult and more important. Some gaps might be easy to resolve with big payoffs for the effort ("low-hanging fruit"), others might take more time and intellect to resolve, while others might be competing gaps. And don't forget that this list might not be static—situations change. So we use needs assessment tools

and techniques to help decision makers prioritize needs in order to guide justifiable choices (Watkins et al., 2012).

- *What are possible solutions to address our needs?* Only when we've answered the questions above should we begin to seriously consider possible solutions to the gaps. These are the activities, programs, projects, policies—the work that we do to address needs. In the education example, *possible* solutions might involve updating standards that new teachers have to meet to receive certification or perhaps working with local colleges to upgrade teacher training programs. The answer could involve any number of possible solutions—and combinations of them. Just as we prioritized gaps earlier, we will want to prioritize solutions.

There are of course more questions to answer in a needs assessment, but these are some of the essential ones that should drive the process, and they apply across individual and organizational performances, private- and public-sector organizations, and domestic and international environments.

Needs Assessment in International Settings

It's hard enough to answer key needs assessment questions working in your own community, country, or culture. It can be even more of a challenge with the added unknowns of working in another country and culture. However, as the world becomes more interconnected, globalization creates opportunities for organizations to enter new territory to further their goals. For businesses, international capabilities can be a crucial competitive advantage, and for governments, academic institutions, nonprofits and other NGOs, increased international efforts mean more likelihood of achieving economic or humanitarian goals.

And this is where evaluators, and other professionals, may be called upon to conduct the assessment of needs in cultures and contexts very different from their own. Usually this is because we bring technical expertise or process experience that the organization values. But without sensitivity to understanding local context, the work may accomplish less than its potential, or do more harm than good. Your assessment might be seen as irrelevant, may be underused, or not used at all.

In a yearlong study about the link between needs assessment and decision making in the humanitarian sector, the Overseas Development Institute (ODI) cited a lack of sufficient needs assessments as a driver of poor decision making (Darcy & Hofmann, 2003). The ODI researchers noted that "the shortage of suitably-qualified assessors is a significant constraint to adequate needs assessment" (Darcy & Hofmann, 2003, p. 69). Similarly, international businesses have noted that a lack of solid planning translates to million- or billion-dollar consequences (see Table 6.1), often due to cultural conflict or a lack of understanding of the local scene (Van der Benk & Rothmann, 2006).

NEW DIRECTIONS FOR EVALUATION • DOI: 10.1002/ev

Table 6.1. The Cost of Insufficient Needs Assessments (and Resulting Poor Decisions)

- An estimated 20–40% of all expatriates sent on foreign assignments cut short their projects or are sent home prematurely (Black & Mendenhall, 1989; Kim & Slocum, 2008).
- Retail giant Walmart failed in the German market because of a poorly designed acquisition strategy and a lack of intercultural competence (including pricing and customer service) and understanding of German laws and regulations (Knorr & Arndt, 2003).
- AlertDriving, an e-learning company, had to spend 18 months and $1 million fixing its mistakes after realizing that its driver training product marketed in Dubai suggested that the center lane of a multilane highway is the safest. In Dubai, the center lane is only for passing (Wooten, 2011).

When working in international contexts, missteps can occur in many parts of the needs assessment process. One example is planning mixed-gender multistakeholder focus groups to reduce the number of focus groups required, and therefore violating cultural norms and inhibiting the resulting data. In Europe or North America you might rely heavily on quantitative data to identify needs, while in other locations qualitative data and dialogue may be more effective tools for reaching consensus. Or, even more subtly, the questions you ask in a needs assessment survey might emphasize individual needs when societal needs take precedence within the culture of concern.

Strategies for International Needs Assessments

The goal of this chapter is to bridge a knowledge gap, empowering needs assessors to avoid problems and achieve better outcomes by sharing strategies to overcome many of the challenges we have observed. To organize this otherwise random list, we are using five-step approach to needs assessments as a framework: Define, Design, Develop, Do, Document.

Step 1: Define. Lay the foundation for a successful assessment.

- *Do your research.* The best thing you can do to begin an international assignment is to start learning immediately as much as you can about the area in which you are to be working. Whether or not there is budget for doing this, the knowledge will pay off dramatically over the course of the project. Begin with Internet, video, or traditional print resources, and schedule coffee dates with anyone you know who has worked in the country. Keep in mind that all of what you read, hear, or see has been created through someone else's cultural lens, and you may find the reality on the ground somewhat different. However, start somewhere and the more input you find, the more likely you are to have a balanced picture.

Table 6.2. Lessons Learned From a Needs Assessment Project in Rwanda (Provided by Dr. Ingrid Guerra-Lopez)

- Identify important cultural customs that could affect the client–consultant relationship and derive a plan for how you will address them in your consulting approach. This can have an impact on many things like trust, participation, and acceptance of recommendations.
- Clarify expectations about participation from various stakeholders, especially as to who will have approval and decision-making power. If you are working with an international development agency, whether directly or through a large contracting firm, you will have to balance their role in participation, review, and approval of the work, as much as the direct client in-country, which may be civil society organizations, their leadership teams, the direct beneficiaries, and/or even government entities.
- Establish clear processes and procedures for ongoing engagement and communication. In many cases, the work will be done through a combination of in-country work and home-based work. It is important to maintain momentum of the work in a way that does not rely solely on your physical presence in the country.

- *Refuse the assignment if you are not a suitable candidate.* As attractive as the project and location might be, there could be others who would be a better fit for this assessment. It would be better to opt out of an activity you cannot perform successfully.
- *Clarify the scope of work and goals of the assessment before traveling to the location.* Often the organizers will not have much experience with needs assessment, so you will often have to refine the scope of work alongside them (see Table 6.2). Use sources such as this issue of *New Directions for Evaluation*, along with those included in the references, to structure the scope of work. Have others review the scope to see if anything is missing, wrong, or to be expanded. You, your clients, and partners must be on the same page with regard to what the assessment can achieve, what exactly you are assessing, the methods to be used, and how results will be reported. Clarity of these issues can, and usually does, get lost in translation between cultures and languages, so be sure to give this phase of project development due attention.
- *Understand the bureaucracy and hierarchies in the location where you will be working.* Americans often take for granted the relatively low levels of informality and directness in our society. But success in many other countries depends on a respect for hierarchies. When working with ministerial agencies, for example, engagement with ministry officials often will be highly orchestrated by lower level staff. As you interact with counterparts at the agency, they will guide you in interactions with upper level decision makers (the minister, vice minister, director general, director, etc.). You'll typically want the vocal support of these higher level officials, so with the guidance of agency counterparts, welcome any opportunities for them to issue a written directive about compliance with an

NEW DIRECTIONS FOR EVALUATION • DOI: 10.1002/ev

assessment and to give a speech to employees and others about its importance, or otherwise promote your work.

Step 2: Design. Design an assessment that guides projects and decisions.

- *Pair up with local experts who speak the language.* Of all recommendations, this will perhaps prove most fruitful. Though local experts may have less experience with needs assessment, strategic planning, monitoring, or evaluation, they will make other valuable contributions, such as sector knowledge, introductions to a local network of technical experts, or relationships with local stakeholder groups. The point is that you should work with local experts, particularly those who have exposure to your culture as well as their own. They will bridge the language and culture gaps for you, carry out much of the "legwork" more efficiently and effectively than you, navigate the bureaucracies, and most importantly, if you listen, redirect you when you are about to make a mistake.
- *Design for a participatory approach to data collection.* If you want your assessment to be used, then it should be informed by those who have the most relevant and useful information. And if you are only talking to the top decision makers, you will likely be ill-informed and could suffer a lack of "buy-in" from those who would be affected. To that end, you'll want to ensure that you have a participatory approach to your assessment. This means looking at the range of possible stakeholders. In the teacher example above, talk to new teachers, experienced ones, teacher trainers from colleges, principals, government education ministry officials from local to national levels, experts in teacher development, parents, students, business people, and so on. It would be a mistake to rely solely on the views of school principals and government officials.
- *Be aware of cultural norms and acceptable behaviors.* Rely on local counterparts to advise you on norms. In some cases you will meet with a village chief or community leader before starting an assessment. Listen closely to the wisdom they impart. For instance, you might not be the right gender or age to interview someone of a different gender or age. Sometimes you may have to work out an alternative arrangement to achieve your goals, such as being accompanied by an authority, a man, a woman, or an elder. You may even have to send someone in your place or find a new path to the information entirely. Do not force your way into a situation that locals tell you is against their culture: It will only harm your assessment and further efforts in the region.
- *Understand the political and economic contexts.* It may be easy to translate from Farsi to English, or yuan to dollars. But consider also the translations around the local nuances of wealth or power. You may want to think about a subject's political position as an Arabic woman in addition to just the Farsi words she says, or factor in the GDP or other local values beyond just a simple currency conversion. Your local experts (monitoring

and evaluation or needs assessment experts, translators, interpreters, and even stakeholders) can help you in the area: Seek their input.

Step 3: Develop. Create useful protocols, instruments, and processes.

- *Consider alternative approaches.* Just as the situation is different from your norm, it may be helpful to use nontraditional methods to complement or substitute for tools that don't fit the context. As an illustration, documentary photographic techniques—placing cameras in the hands of stakeholders for participatory, visual assessment—have helped break barriers of language, race, and gender (Wang & Burris, 1997). Crowdsourcing techniques for engaging a large number of stakeholders (e.g., calling for public input via social media) can also make your assessment more robust and reduce the influence of any perspectives or biases that may come from being an outsider to the environment.
- *Learn from those who have come before you.* Learn as much as possible about projects that have preceded your work in regard to challenges, successes, problem-solving approaches, and failures. Resources could include:
  - World Bank documents and reports (collected at http://documents. worldbank.org; particularly implementation and completion reports or those done by Independent Evaluation Group at http://ieg.worldbankgroup.org).
  - USAID evaluations (www.usaid.gov/evaluation).
  - Loma Linda University collection of International and Cross-Cultural Resources (includes variety of backgrounds, guides, fact sheets, customs and etiquette notes, etc.—most generated for government or NGO worker use at http://libguides.llu.edu/internationalculture).
  - Other resources are available through organizations including United Nations, Inter-American Development Bank, Asia Development Bank, and OECD.
- *If you don't speak the local language, be sure to plan and budget for translation and interpretation help.* Often there will be key documents to read in order to do the assessment. First, you will have to determine—through consultation with others—what those documents might be. Next, proper translation will be important, and that takes time and money. Whenever possible, seek translators who have exposure to your culture, your language, as well as the technical language of the context for which the assessment is being done. The more truly they understand both cultures, the better they will be suited to convey meaning and raise flags to possible cultural miscommunications.

  You should also budget for the review of the translation, as the quality of work can vary widely. In addition, for any interviews, meetings, and other interactions that you will conduct, plan ahead for interpretation services. Ideally, your interpreter and translator is the same person, or

Table 6.3. Lessons Learned From a Needs Assessment Project in Russia (Provided by Dr. Ingrid Guerra-Lopez)

- Determine the logistical requirements for conducting the work as smoothly as possible. Will you require a simultaneous translator? Is it better to have someone who speaks the local language(s) as part of your core team? How will you get around? Is there a culturally appropriate order in which you must establish your meetings/interviews?
- If one of the overarching goals of the project is to build capacity, use participatory and coaching approaches as much as possible in your work. It is important to conduct the project in a way that transfers skills to local teams and the client. It is the most effective way of supporting sustainable change. You want to avoid providing consulting reports and other development project deliverables that will be filed somewhere never to be seen again, because the clients were not part of their development and do not understand the logic of such deliverables. We should do assessments *with* our international development partners and clients rather than do assessment *for* them.

you will have a team who work together with you and your team (see Table 6.3).

Step 4: Do. Manage the implementation of your international needs assessment.

- *If customary, bring small gifts.* In many cultures it is customary to bring small gifts (typically of little financial value) for those with whom you are meeting. If this is a norm in the places you will be working, bring small gifts with you.
- *Be aware of technology opportunities and limitations.* Access and comfort with technology varies widely around the globe. Conduct your assessment using the technology tools that make the most sense for your participants. You might be surprised by opportunities to use technology. Weekly or monthly household surveys, for example, in some countries are now conducted via cell phone—saving time and resources. Conversely, while online surveys are common, they may not be valuable in some contexts where participants are less comfortable with technology. If you do use technology, pilot it with several representative participants before implementing.

Step 5: Document. Report your findings and make improvements for your next assessment.

- *Consider the best etiquette for documentation.* Ask stakeholders in your needs assessment what is the best way to record interviews, focus groups, or performance observations. There are options available and you should select the one(s) that will ensure the validity (minimally influence what participants say or do) of your data and provide you with the most accurate record possible for the situation. Consider taking notes yourself or

NEW DIRECTIONS FOR EVALUATION • DOI: 10.1002/ev

having a second person from the local area take notes for you. If appropriate, record the assessment using an audio and video recorder.

- *Communicate.* Have a communications plan that you enact throughout your assessment. It is important that it fits well with the environment in which you are working. Ask stakeholders early on about their expectations. Do they want weekly updates by email, a formal report at the end, or a wiki where they can contribute to the assessment as it is being conducted? Each context requires a different mix of communications. Possible communications channels include:
  - Formal report
  - Summary report
  - Presentation
  - Webinar
  - Website
  - Blog or wiki
  - Social media (Twitter, Facebook, WeShareScience, etc.)
  - Email updates
  - Conference calls

Needs Assessment Capacity

We have covered some of the challenges with needs assessments in an international context and the negative results from some initiatives that weren't well planned. In acknowledgment of the importance of needs assessments and their common pitfalls, a movement toward adaptive project management has gained ground, featuring in part an increased link between planning and evaluation. For example, the United States Agency for International Aid (USAID) with its "Collaborating, Learning, and Adapting" initiative and the World Bank with its "Science of Delivery" approach aim to build needs assessment and evaluation more tightly into project formulation, design, and delivery.

One challenge with these large-scale initiatives is the relatively limited global capacity for conducting needs assessments. The number of professionals skilled at conducting needs assessment is far lower than that required for conducting quality evaluations, and there are almost no systems in place to build that capacity. So far, there are two major implications of this status on the practice: (a) a small number of mostly American needs assessment professionals have struggled to serve diverse international demand for conducting assessments, and (b) due to a lack of capacity, many such assessments are done by professionals with little or no training in conducting them, limiting the value of the results.

One way to improve is to increase the capacity of "local" professionals to conduct quality needs assessments. Institutions should enhance the in-region or in-country ability with regard to the needs assessment capacity of "local" professionals. This could be done in partnership

New Directions for Evaluation • DOI: 10.1002/ev

with those doing similar capacity building relative to evaluation (e.g., www.theclearinitiative.org), since both share many similar approaches to design, data collection, and analysis. In addition, given the alignment of needs assessments with strategic planning, capacity development for effective planning could be integrated into the dialogue and activities.

Still, professionals conducting needs assessments in international context must be aware of, and address, the complex issues presented previously. Within the field of needs assessment, we recognize that there is not a large literature base to guide international practice. The guidance given here came from the experiences by those who have been learning, often rather unsystematically, on the job. With the globalization and the demand for international development to do more with less, improving the quality of international needs assessment practices is critical.

Summary

It is not that we must change our models or approaches when conducting needs assessments in international contexts. Rather, it is that we frequently have to vary how we apply our tools in new and unfamiliar settings. It could be as simple as collaborating with a local evaluator, or as complex as collecting and analyzing data across multiple languages and dialects. While international needs assessments vary greatly, based on our experiences we have offered valuable lessons learned that can hopefully help you avoid some of the missteps we have made over the years—allowing your assessments to live up to their potential in situations where scarce resources require that we be extra careful in practice.

References

Altschuld, J. W. (2010). *The needs assessment kit.* Thousand Oaks, CA: Sage.
Black, J., & Mendenhall, M. (1989). A practical but theory-based framework for selecting cross-cultural training methods. *Human Resources Management, 28,* 511–539.
Darcy, J., & Hofmann, C. (2003). *According to need? Needs assessment and decision-making in the humanitarian sector.* London, UK: Humanitarian Policy Group, Overseas Development Institute.
Kaufman, R. (2011). *A manager's pocket guide to strategic thinking and planning.* Amherst, MA: HRD Press.
Kaufman, R., & Guerra-Lopez, I. (2013). *Needs assessment for organizational success.* Alexandria, VA: ASTD Press.
Kim, K., & Slocum, J. (2008). Individual differences and expatriate assignment effectiveness: The case of U.S.-based Korean expatriates. *Journal of World Business, 43*(1), 109–126.
Knorr, A., & Arndt, A. (2003). *Why did Wal-Mart fail in Germany?* Breman, Germany: Institut für Weltwirtschaft und Internationales Management. Retrieved from http://www.iwim.uni-bremen.de/publikationen/pdf/w024.pdf
United Nations Millennium Project. (2004). *Millennium development goals needs assessments: Country case studies of Bangladesh, Cambodia, Ghana, Tanzania*

and Uganda (Working Paper). Retrieved from http://www.unmillenniumproject.org/documents/mp_ccspaper_jan1704.pdf

Van der Benk, M., & Rothmann, S. (2006). Correlates of expatriates' cross-cultural adjustment. *Management Dynamics, 15*(4), 29–39.

Wang, C., & Burris, M. (1997). Photovoice: Concept, methodology, and use for participatory needs assessment. *Health Education & Behavior, 24*(3), 369–387.

Watkins, R., West Meiers, M., & Visser, Y. (2012). *A Guide to assessing needs: Essential tools for collecting information, making decisions, and achieving development results.* Washington, DC: The World Bank.

Wooten, A. (2011). Failure to adapt international e-learning can cost millions. *Deseret News.* Retrieved from http://www.deseretnews.com/article/705374213/Failure-to-adapt-international-e-learning-can-cost-millions.html?pg=all

MAURYA WEST MEIERS *is an evaluation officer with the Internal Evaluation Group at the World Bank and an author of* A Guide to Assessing Needs.

RYAN WATKINS *is an associate professor at George Washington University in Washington, DC, and founder of www.NeedsAssessment.org and www.WeShareScience.com.*

KRISTIN MARSH SONG *is a senior consultant with Booz Allen Hamilton, working in Learning Analysis and Development.*

Altschuld, J. W., Hung, H.-L., & Lee, Y.-F. (2014). Needs assessment and asset/capacity building: A promising development in practice. In J. W. Altschuld & R. Watkins (Eds.), *Needs
assessment: Trends and a view toward the future. New Directions for Evaluation, 144,* 89–103.

7

Needs Assessment and Asset/Capacity Building: A Promising Development in Practice

James W. Altschuld, Hsin-Ling (Sonya) Hung, Yi-Fang Lee

Abstract

*From time to time there have been sharp and barbed criticisms of needs
assessment—for example, starting from a deficit perspective (a potentially negative view based on problems and issues) as opposed to an asset-based perspective (a more positive view based on strengths and resources). In the last 10–15
years, this has led to a hybrid model of asset/capacity building and needs assessment that is increasingly noticeable in community improvement, public safety,
health, and other similar projects. Needs assessment and asset/capacity building are compared and contrasted in this chapter as a premise for synthesizing
the new hybrid approach. The steps necessary for making the hybrid come to
life are explained in some detail, as well as a few methods that might be used in
implementing it. Two current examples of hybrid studies are analyzed, followed
by implications of and issues inherent in following this new course of action.
© Wiley Periodicals, Inc., and the American Evaluation Association.*

An Introduction to Asset/Capacity Building

Why is the combined practice of needs assessment (NA) and asset/capacity
building (A/CB) beginning to appear in the literature? Since the early days
of modern needs assessment, there has been a steady stream of criticism
on a solely needs-focused approach. It was sharply attacked by Kretzmann

and Mcknight in their 1993 seminal work "Building Communities From the Inside Out." They were opposed to planning for improvement and change in social programs from a needs-only approach—as contrasted to starting from assets and strengths. At the same time, appreciative inquiry was developing as a method for applying asset/capacity building in practical ways. Other fields, such as positivist psychology, were also looking at new approaches to what was being done; and in development economics, Sen's (1989) work in capability economics earned him a Nobel Prize.

For many, needs start from discrepancies rather than a positive asset and resource foundation. Needs represent what is wrong or missing, a deficit is to be overcome, and corrections must be made. This negative feel is noticeable even though needs do get into solution strategies and resources (assets) for resolving problems, but assets are always viewed in terms of gaps not as the beginning of work on program development.

The critics have noted that assessing needs has not always led to significant developments in health, education, government, and other areas. The record of NA in regard to productivity is not distinguished, and, in impoverished communities, it can promote a sense of dependency that will tend to leave those communities always in poor condition. For example, organizations may quickly look for funds and resources (or turn to others or governmental agencies) when they come from a needs perspective, not from one where they look at what they can do for themselves. In contrast, when communities note their strengths and what they bring to the table, they can be enabled to move forward in many situations.

So do you focus on positives or negatives? Do needs versus assets/resources/strengths have to be polar opposites (see Figure 7.1)? Besides philosophical differences, other concerns have been raised about needs-only approaches such as they often rely on social indicators in databases than a more humanistic and holistic sense of what is on the mind of communities and/or organizations. They have been portrayed as cold and stark, and not getting down to the level of people and what they value (Altschuld, 2014).

The Needs Assessment Counterpoint

In response to the early attacks, Kamis (1979) and Witkin (1988, 1992) agreed that the criticisms had validity and that assessments would be enhanced and benefit from the voice of the people. Data collection should be upgraded and there was (and still is) a press to have better instruments (Altschuld, 2004). In addition, it has been stressed that soft and hard methods must work in concert (Altschuld, Hung, & Lee, 2013).

On the other hand, some concerns of early critiques were off target—more about the implementation of assessment than identifying needs and utilizing that information to plan programs—and in many applications, individuals and constituencies have not just been providers of data, but full

Figure 7.1. Thesis, Antithesis, and Synthesis (Based on Altschuld, 2014)

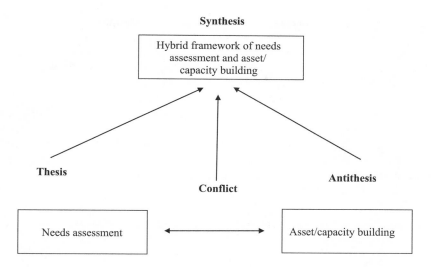

partners in pre- and postassessment decision making. Moreover, learning about assets and strengths was tacitly integrated into design when not explicitly present. Inferring from these experiences, perhaps the two ends of the needs-versus-assets spectrum overlap to a higher degree than apparent upon first glance.

Altschuld (2014) proposed that differences between needs assessment and asset/capacity building are not extreme, and a synergism across them is appropriate and worthwhile. To examine this assertion, we must define asset/capacity building and needs assessment, compare them, and offer a hybrid framework for doing the two in tandem. Then, does the hybrid fit the real world and to what extent and how well do actual cases demonstrate its principles? (The remainder of this discussion is based heavily on Altschuld, 2014 and partly on Altschuld et al., 2013.)

Asset/Capacity Building and Needs Assessment: Definitions and Comparisons

Asset/capacity building is intended to embed a mindset in an organization or community to utilize its strengths for growth and improvement. It does this by identifying resources, social structures, people, and existing programs that become the basis for change. How can we capitalize and take advantage of what we have; how can we leverage off of what is there?

Specifically, A/CB is about locating and cataloging the assets (organization, community, agency, fiscal, skills of individual people) available or potentially available to a group and using that knowledge to move the group ahead in a positive way (Altschuld, 2014). The assumption is that the community or organization is in control of (at least has influence on) the process and determines how assets, strengths, and resources should be put to work. Other individuals may be involved in the assessment, but the community is in charge of its destiny. Engaging in A/CB can help a group to proceed forward and become more resilient via internal leadership.

Whereas a "need is a problem that should be attended to or resolved" (Altschuld & Kumar, 2010, p. 3), "it is a gap or discrepancy between 'the what should be' and 'the what is' conditions. Needs assessments consist of identifying discrepancies, prioritizing them, making needs-based decisions, allocating resources, and implementing actions in organizations to resolve important needs" (p. 20). As Watkins and Kavale (Chapter 2 of this issue) note, the deficit definition has an impact on what gets measured as well as recommendations that may come from an assessment.

Comparisons of Asset/Capacity Building and Needs Assessment

In Table 7.1, A/CB and NA are compared. Many of the differences are of degree rather than kind, and the degree is not always that large. Notably, the premise of activities, the role of facilitators or leaders, and the contexts have enough similarities pointing toward a possible merger of the two into a hybrid framework. If the hybrid is complementary, it could go beyond what needs assessment or A/CB could individually accomplish.

With regard to A/CB, what is found about strengths avoids the taint of discrepancy thinking. Having the needs known at the same time could be useful for how to best apply assets. For NA, it can be invigorating to open up to a "can do" attitude and clarify what is already working. The idea is to blend concepts in a manner that is illuminative without favoring needs or assets. A hybrid approach should preserve to the extent possible the underlying philosophies so that each is considered honestly without bias.

A Hybrid Needs Assessment and A/CB Framework

At its core, a new hybrid must determine needs and assets in independent yet intertwined ways. It has to be open to the two perspectives and responsive to the voices and guidance of the community or group(s) involved. It should be empowering, not dependency-oriented, and use multiple methods for data collection. The hybrid approach should also include aspects of empowerment evaluation, evaluation capacity building, and address the strengths, weaknesses, opportunities, and threats (SWOT) components of strategic planning. A synthesized eight-step process is provided in Table 7.2. It also has roots in Witkin's (1984) three phases of NA, as updated by Altschuld and Kumar (2010).

Table 7.1. Comparison of A/CB and NA on a Number of Dimensions

Asset/Capacity Building	Dimension	Needs Assessment
Begins with identifying assets and strengths from a self-reliant stance	Premise of the activity	Starting with needs (discrepancies, gaps in performance) as the basis for action, determine the "what should be" and the "what is" conditions and gaps between them
Facilitators are catalysts for the community or organization to find its own direction for capitalizing on assets and strengths; the group itself is ready to lead the endeavor	Role of external individuals	Initially, more often externally led in what is studied The organization or community may be involved early via a needs assessment committee (NAC), which makes many decisions about focus
A/CB is usually in public health, community development, etc.	Context	Needs assessments are in agencies, businesses, organizations, institutions, and companies; the context is narrower and less complex than communities
In A/CB, a group in a community have a sense that change is required	How the work might begin?	Similar to A/CB but may be more in response to problems; impetus may come from the administrative level
Qualitative methods—interviews, observations, focus groups, photovoice, etc.—predominate Not much into causal analysis or prioritization strategies	Methodology focus	Surveys, database analyses noticeable in the past; multiple methods emphasized now More method variety than A/CB including causal analysis and prioritization
The community may define what data are collected and do the data collection	Who is or what groups are involved in data collection?	As needs assessment begins, the assessor usually does more of this, but if a NAC is involved, it may be similar to A/CB
Primarily the community and groups and may include looking at the physical environment	From what individuals or groups are data obtained?	Data is from three levels: direct recipients of services, providers of services (teachers, health workers), and the management

(Continued)

Table 7.1. Continued

Asset/Capacity Building	Dimension	Needs Assessment
Community discussions about future steps/directions and even interpretation of the data	Use of results	Identify the most important discrepancies for prioritization and causal analysis for next actions The needs assessor with the NAC would usually do the above steps
Time depends on what has been learned and future efforts to be undertaken; usually longer than a needs assessment (see below)	Time frame	For smaller, less severe needs, the estimate would be three months, not including implementation of solutions For major and severe needs, the time would be longer
Cooperation and collaboration are essential with collaboration (shared vision, input, decision making) more intense than cooperation and requiring tradeoffs for communities	Role of collaboration and/or cooperation	There are cooperative and collaborative needs assessments; some overlap with A/CB

Table 7.2. A Hybrid Process Framework (For a Detailed Discussion of the Table, see Altschuld, 2014)

Step	Purpose	Comments
1. Scoping the context	Find basic information about needs and assets, or a hybrid	Form a working committee to find the information
2. Decide on what actions should be taken	Decide what to do—nothing, a needs assessment, asset/capacity building, or a hybrid procedure	The community/working committee, not an external person or group, makes the decision
3. Divide the working group into two subcommittees	Identify resources, strengths, and assets and needs at the same time; subcommittees work *independently* on one or the other	Charge to each subcommittee must be clear; if the group is not large enough for division, start with the asset (positive) side of the equation
4. Committees *independently* put key findings in tables or figures	Portray findings in formats that facilitate discussion about what has been learned	Tables/simple figures enable decision making; too much data can overwhelm, strive for simplicity
5. Subcommittee(s) exchange findings and discuss how to use results	Align assets and resources with needs; come to agreement as to where they could be applied to resolve needs, but only if they are congruent	Good understanding of needs and assets generated and arrayed to promote discourse; each subcommittee should review the work of the other before discussing
6. Develop a strategy for improvement based on assets and needs	Translate step 5 into mechanisms for positive change	The information establishes a foundation for action plans
7. Implement, monitor, evaluate improvement strategy	Implement activities, see how they are functioning, and what the outcomes are	Determine that plans are translated into actuality; formative and summative evaluation are done
8. Go back to step 1, add more areas to the improvement package	Pick up other facets of improvement that could not be done initially	Usually there are too many areas to proceed, so revisit previous results; move ahead with selected ones

The Assets Rubric

Identifying assets may seem straightforward, but deeper thought typically reveals complexity. Suppose you had to find and catalog resources in a state for adults with physical disabilities, persons requiring mental health assistance, veterans returning from wars, and others to help them live independently. They span age ranges and must cope with issues involving housing, employment, vocational guidance, transportation, and job training. The potential population comes from urban and rural (with their own special demands) areas. For assets and resources, you would think of organizations at state and local levels, state and municipal agencies, private entities, social services, and others whose missions relate to the concerns of interest.

That just scratches the surface, however. Educational and health providers are part of the picture, as are services offered through offices of veterans' affairs. Also, we cannot neglect what family members (neighbors) contribute that comes from their caring. It is valuable and significant but under the radar, and hard to catalog and fully describe once determined. Other assets are collaborations and cooperation across individuals, agencies, religious institutions, and the like. These linkages may be a strong part of assets but akin to contributions from individuals they are often latent and difficult to discern.

Learning about resources and assets could be more complicated and time consuming than learning about needs. The state level example above may not totally pertain to your context or to community development in a section of a city or for a smaller endeavor, such as in an organization or business, but the investigation can be scaled down. The challenge is how do you begin to find out about strengths, assets, and resources?

Start simply with reconnaissance. Ask people within the system about resources and where they go to find support. What groups do they turn to, what have they used before, and what are the skills in the organization or system? This information can come from interviews or short surveys. Or drive through the community to observe what is there or not there—a kind of microethnography. Go to community meetings, hear what people are saying. Find "gatekeepers" who have insights into a community or social environment. In a city they are realtors, police, firefighters, clergy, educational leaders, and others who sense the heartbeat and pulse of what is happening.

Usually classes (or categories) of assets and strengths are helpful for organizing the study. Kretzmann and McKnight (1993) suggest a map of community assets divided into local institutions (schools, libraries, businesses, etc.), citizen associations (churches, cultural groups, and others), and the gifts, talents, and special skills of individuals. In the latter might be youth, senior citizens, skilled workers, artists, and people with talents and skills. It is important to see if there are tangible working relationships across groups, as well as a spirit of cooperation and a volunteer ethos in a community. As resources are located, they are cataloged, collated, and arrayed (mapped) in a manner to facilitate decision making.

It is natural to want to align resources and assets with needs right away (what they are doing in the accounting department could help us improve productivity here in the billing department), but it is recommended to think of assets in their own right first by viewing them separately from needs. This might lead to innovation outside of the narrower confines of needs. Such openness is encouraged in hybrid work when the two approaches are connected but not linked tightly. Based on experience it is useful to keep this separation until you reach the point where you must combine them to make recommendations regarding what to do next.

Some Notes About Methods for Determining Assets

Numerous methods are used for needs assessments; common ones are surveys, interviews, and epidemiological analyses. These are well known; they will not be covered here, and it is not a stretch to tweak the first two for asset identification. Through informal interviews we could, for instance, randomly query some individuals about problems and issues (needs) and others about assets, strengths, and things that are good about the community. Likewise, other methods borrowed from needs assessment, and evaluation, can be applied to A/CB initiatives.

One is a form of community-based participatory research or a rapid appraisal technique usually implemented by individuals selected from the community (local students, senior citizens, or other volunteers) and trained to do the interviews. Since they are of the community, they have better rapport and "street creds" than external interviewers. Five to ten of them can quickly do short interviews with a sizable number of community members about strengths and needs. Sampling is not random but could be across the demographics of the locality. This has proved to be effective and fast for obtaining a snapshot of a community's views. If more data are required, simply interview a few more people for confirmation or expansion. Data from other sources (records, prior reports) also would be used for confirmation.

Another interesting technique for A/CB is photovoice. Community members take pictures of the strengths and problems in the environment. They are given some but minimal guidance so as to not influence what they photograph and provided with inexpensive, disposable cameras or use cell phones. The pictures are shared (posted on a wall) in a work session, grouped together if appropriate, discussed at length, and then the photographers caption them and write short explanatory paragraphs or narratives. The photos become the focal point for a large community/organizational meeting where everyone engages in reviewing them and offering their opinion.

The procedure gives voice (or vision in this case) to people from the community, with limited input from those conducting the assessment. It is usually best to have done surveys, looked at government facts, and collected additional information to complement what has been found by the photographers. Photovoice may be better for smaller communities than larger ones where sampling can be a major issue.

Case Studies of Hybrid Implementation

To date, most uses of a hybrid framework of needs assessment and A/CB have been in public health and community development. The training of those in public health and social work may account for this. Still, the principles of hybrid work should, over time, transfer to other areas of practice (evaluation, education, and business). We sought examples that viewed assessing needs and assets as related yet independent entities, did not compromise either one, used multiple methods, and had the locus of control (to the extent feasible) residing in the community or organization. We looked for applications where the perspectives of people are collected and affect subsequent decisions. These ingredients are all necessary for a hybrid; if not evident and in balance, the activity would favor needs assessment or A/CB over the other.

Two cases are provided in Exhibits 7.1 and 7.2. It should be stressed that there is no perfect hybrid—all have similarities and special features. The two that are described are distinct in the evaluative nature of what was implemented in one instance and of the cultural sensitivity in the other. Both exhibits are summaries of what was done and quite detailed. Their purpose here is to show what it takes to implement a hybrid approach for complex social problems.

Across the Cases

A cursory glance at the descriptions in the two exhibits reveals that they are more involved than doing a needs assessment or a looking at assets as stand-alone activities. Second, in each instance, the involved staff clearly recognized the underlying philosophies of needs assessment and A/CB. Notably, in the Native American investigation (Exhibit 7.2), they commented about the differences among them and that identifying assets and strengths took priority over the assessment of needs. Inferring from the cultural aspect of that work, the "can do" positive attitude was reinforced, without which the project might not have been successful.

Third, obviously multiple methods were used in both investigations. Such practice might be part of an ordinary needs assessment but generally not so much for learning about resources and strengths. Exploring both needs and assets embeds both these efforts in the hybrid realm. Fourth, the stance of the outsiders is facilitative, not controlling, which is part of hybrid endeavors. This is mentioned in Exhibit 7.1 in relation to the role of staff: as shown in Exhibit 7.2, staff members were along for the ride, being

Exhibit 7.1. The Case of Community Development in Barcelona, Spain (Fuertes et al., 2012)

Background and what was done
  Health care in two deprived areas of Barcelona
  Guiding Community Action Model (three parts)
    Alliances with stakeholders/members of the community
    Participatory needs and asset assessment
    Plan, implement, and evaluate interventions
  Use the model, evaluate each of its three main features via 18 indicators
  Community participation in health decisions important to enhance outcomes
  Rich connections across many sectors and groups
  Needs/asset assessments (variety of data)
    Quantitative and qualitative data
    Participative prioritization of needs and inventory of assets and resources
  Evaluation
    Consensus on objectives
    Literature review of effective interventions
    Use existing (or develop new) evaluation procedures
    Prioritize how to evaluate
    Do the evaluation
  Eighteen indicators for the three parts of the model (number of meetings of working group, satisfaction surveys, demographics of users, and other evaluation strategies)

Highlighted results
  Eighteen indicators assessed across the two areas of the city
  Particularly high achievement for the first two model parts on most indicators
  Some drop off but reasonable results for intervention implementation in one of the two city areas

Other observations
  Involved staff promoted and used the voice of the people
  Participation of the community
    Empowered
    Involved in meetings
    Part of decision making
    Increased visibility of interventions
    Overall approach was deemed feasible

Exhibit 7.2. The Case of an External Group Being Culturally Sensitive to a Local Population (Fisher & Ball, 2002)

Background

    Tribal communities and ways of doing needs/asset assessments

    External university group had to establish a meaningful, utilitarian partnership

    Resulting partnership could be a guide for others

    Take advantage of what indigenous communities had done before but never formally recorded in regard to health issues, strengths, and resources already available in the locality

    Outsiders must be sensitive to the native culture but don't patronize

    Use information to develop culturally grounded health interventions

    Let the research agenda emerge, a predetermined one would fail as in the past

      Recognize tribal sovereignty

      Communicate results and keep community involved

      Some negative history regarding outsiders had to be overcome

Methods

    Community-based participatory research was adopted for the Tribal Participatory Research Model (Fisher & Ball, 2002, 2003)

    Balance what the community can provide as tied into issues to be dealt with *but* do not overemphasize/treat issues as a pathology; keep the positive focus of asset/capacity building

      Youth substance abuse was the key concern

    Think partnership, do not see the community as "subjects"

    Best if the investigators are invited into the community which was the case here

Objectives

    Identify/prioritize health issues of greatest community concern

    Do the same for strengths and resources related to the issues

    Develop community-based, relevant interventions and pilot test them

    Be open to other issues that may arise

    Key stakeholder interviews used (examples of questions provided)

    Focus group interviews ($n = 4$) employed to help understand the data

(Continued)

Exhibit 7.2. Continued

Highlighted results
Prioritized list of health problems
Community strengths and assets identified
Community as the expert partner and key decision maker
Interventions tied to community norms

Discussion by the researchers
Became part of the journey (going native may fit)
Process can be slow but is worth it
Sense of and in-depth, not superficial community involvement
Concluded with 14 lessons learned (all are valuable with one being it is essential to be strength as opposed to problem-focused)

learners on the journey rather than conducting it. Community/organization empowerment is critical and was in abundance in the two studies as was the *voice of the people*.

The hybrid rests on people—not someone else—influencing their collective destiny and determining their fate and directions for progress. A needs assessment and A/CB venture don't make sense without this; the external consultants were respectful of the communities with which they were interacting. Their understanding was what was needed for the desired impact and they are to be commended for their professionalism and thoughtfulness.

A Few Points to Ponder

Time and cost will factor into any hybrid project. It takes longer to collect data about assets and needs, digest results from mixed methods, apply multiple skill sets for data collection, analyze and interpret results, blend findings so that meaning is derived across them, and translate the knowledge gained into policies and intervention strategies that benefit communities and organizations. This isn't a small undertaking, nor one to be undertaken lightly. It demands patience on the part of involved communities and those facilitating them. Communications to keep activities flowing smoothly will be greater than in most projects. Maturation (à la Campbell and Stanley) as a source of invalidity could affect an effort in a negative direction. This is not to deter anyone from conducting a hybrid approach but to make certain that it is done with eyes wide open as to what might happen and be required. Budgeting sufficient time and resources for the job, maintaining contacts, and keeping channels open should be included in project plans and finances.

Another point comes from an observation of what is not in the literature. Most publications where needs assessment and asset identification have been implemented simultaneously consist of descriptions of what has taken place, perceptions of how well they worked, and reflections from those outside of the community. These have been excellent and informative, but there is not much research about hybrid usage. In that regard, what about focus group interviews of community members regarding perceptions of the process? What did they think about how decisions were made, was the community improved or was there the potential for improvement, did they ever get bored and frustrated with the process, did they ever think of quitting, were all segments of the community really contacted and were their opinions collected and utilized, what should their role be, would they commit to another project like this in the future, and other relevant questions?

In addition, what information is best given the time, funds, and personnel that are required in order to learn about assets and needs and the facilitation of hybrid endeavors? This work can be intensive. Are some sources better than others, and what would be the cost-efficient ways to obtain data? Lastly, facilitation in complex settings is a delicate, critical dance with balance being mandatory. How do we do this, when do we back away, and when do we gently and tactfully prod and push? An appropriate equilibrium must be realized and can lead to great reward if handled appropriately. More guidance from the field would be very useful.

References

Altschuld, J. W. (2004). Emerging dimensions of needs assessment. *Performance Improvement*, 43(1), 10–15.

Altschuld, J. W. (2014). *Bridging the gap between asset/capacity building and needs assessment*. Thousand Oaks, CA: Sage.

Altschuld, J. W., Hung, H.-L., & Lee, Y.-F. (2013, October). *Linking asset and needs assessment: Identifying assets*. Skill-building workshop presented at the annual meeting of the American Evaluation Association, Washington, DC.

Altschuld, J. W., & Kumar, D. D. (2010). *Needs assessment: An overview* (Needs Assessment Kit 1). Thousand Oaks, CA: Sage.

Fisher, P. A., & Ball, T. J. (2002). The Indian family wellness project: An application of the tribal participatory research model. *Prevention Science*, 3(3), 235–240.

Fisher, P. A., & Ball, T. J. (2003). Tribal participatory research: Mechanisms of a collaborative model. *American Journal of Community psychology*, 32(3–4), 207–216.

Fuertes, C., Pasarín, M. I., Borrell, C., Artazcoz, L., Díez, È., & the Group of Health in the Neighborhoods. (2012). Feasibility of a community action model oriented to reduce inequalities in health. *Health Policy*, 107(2–3), 289–295. doi:10.1016/j.healthpol.2012.06.001

Kamis, E. (1979). A witness for the defense of need assessment. *Evaluation and Program Planning*, 2(1), 7–12.

Kretzmann, J. P., & McKnight, J. L. (1993). *Building communities from the inside out*. Chicago, IL: ACTA Publications.

Sen, A. (1989). Development as capability expansion. *Journal of Development Planning*, 19, 41–58.

Thomas, L. R., Donovan, D. M., & Sigo, R. L. W. (2010). Identifying community needs and resources in a native community: A research partnership in the pacific northwest. *International Journal of Mental Health and Addiction*, 8(2), 362–373. doi:10.1007/s11469–009–9233–1

Witkin, B. R. (1984). *Assessing needs in educational and social programs: Using information to make decisions, set priorities, and allocate resources*. San Francisco, CA: Jossey-Bass.

Witkin, B. R. (1988). To the editor. *Educational Planning*, 7(2), 3–4.

Witkin, B. R. (1992). Is this trip necessary? Needs assessment: A personal memoir and reappraisal. *Educational Planning*, 8(2), 13–33.

James W. Altschuld is professor emeritus in the College of Education and Human Ecology, The Ohio State University.

Hsin-Ling (Sonya) Hung is an assistant professor in the Department of Educational Foundations and Research at the University of North Dakota.

Yi-Fang Lee is a professor in the Department of Industrial Education at National Taiwan Normal University.

Watkins, R., & Altschuld, J. M. (2014). A final note about improving needs assessment research and practice. In J. W. Altschuld& R. Watkins (Eds.), *Needs assessment: Trends and a view toward the future. New Directions for Evaluation, 144*, 105–114.

8

A Final Note About Improving Needs Assessment Research and Practice

Ryan Watkins, James W. Altschuld

Abstract

As with any field of inquiry and application, needs assessment is an evolving topic of research and practice. The theories, models, tools, and approaches are not idle targets. In this chapter, the authors explore the emerging trends and issues of the field, suggesting elements of an exciting future and the continuing call for more research that can improve practice. They include an examination of how technologies are expanding the methods employed in assessments and a discussion of how many of the challenges that have nagged at assessors for decades continue to limit our results. The future for needs assessments remains bright, but much work remains to be done in order for needs assessment to mature as a field. © Wiley Periodicals, Inc., and the American Evaluation Association.

Introduction

We would be remiss if we did not close this issue with a few observations about the alignment of research, theory, and practice in needs assessment methods. The landscape of needs assessment has been changing (as described in Chapter 1), as is likely most evident in the methods being applied today. Epidemiological-type studies, for instance, appear more frequently with the advent of "big data." At the same time, almost paradoxically, the number of qualitative techniques being applied to probe deeply into situations has been growing as well. Technology is also creating new updates to assessment data collection methods, such as cyber meetings, on-line focus groups, photovoice, rapid participatory appraisal, real-time surveys, and other possibilities. In this chapter, we will explore some of these new opportunities and speculate as to what needs assessment could look like methodologically in the future.

Evolving Methods

In 1979, Kamis-Gould called on professionals to do a better job of measuring needs. More than a decade later, Witkin (1994) supported that call to action, and in 2010 Altschuld (see Altschuld & White, 2010; White & Altschuld, 2012) again called for more research and investigation into assessment methods. This continuing mandate to improve techniques for assessing needs is a reflection of insufficient research being done and the evolving options available to assessors.

In the 21st century, we have more choices than ever before. As discussed in Chapter 2, the definition of *needs*, and in turn *needs assessment*, should guide the choice of methods rather than the reverse of letting the methods we prefer shape the needs we assess. In other words, don't enter an assessment with the method picked a priori. Instead, define the needs to be assessed and then select appropriate ways for measuring them, which may include many different approaches. Flipping the initial focus from how (methods) to what (needs) is essential for understanding when to use the variety of available procedures and what results you can expect from your work.

In the field of needs assessment, there is a particularly close relationship between practice, theory, tools, and techniques. With practice informing theory and vice versa, leaders in the field have frequently had one foot in practice and one in the academy. This has led to a dynamic set of tools for needs assessment, with many borrowed and customized from other fields. For example, needs assessments are frequently integrated in strategic planning initiatives, with tools such as Future Search (Weisbord & Janoff, 2009) and SWOT (Leigh, 2009) employed to assist in specifying the "desired" state in terms of results. Likewise, multidisciplinary tools such as surveys have been tailored for needs assessments to utilize dual- and triple-response scales to collect data on needs as gaps (see Altschuld, 2010; Kaufman, Guerra-Lopez, Watkins, & Leigh, 2008).

In the future, we anticipate that we will see more of this, with newer techniques (such as photovoice, crowdsourcing, or "big data" analysis) being adapted for needs assessment purposes. Many of these techniques are due to new technologies making it possible for assessors to fit them into varied practical contexts. Technologies (from the spread of smartphone apps and broadband access to Web 2.0 tools and new qualitative data analysis software) provide opportunities to improve what we do from designing and developing to implementing and disseminating results. As examples, Skype

NEW DIRECTIONS FOR EVALUATION • DOI: 10.1002/ev

or Google Hangouts are free tools that assessors can use to engage with stakeholders who may not be available in person (e.g., Google Hangouts allows for video calls with up to nine participants). Likewise, SurveyMonkey and related online survey tools now make it faster and easier to collect data from people regardless of location, and SMS text surveys are often used in international development contexts. These illustrate how technology provides more choices; next are major trends that we believe will continue to shape how needs assessments are done.

Big Data and Real-Time Data

The amount of data that is now available for needs assessment has grown rapidly in the last two decades. From detailed data on customer behavior to real-time data on market prices collected by cell phones, there is increasingly more information for decisions. Analyzing, interpreting, and using that data are all challenges (and opportunities) for needs assessments. And it is easy to get overwhelmed by the sheer number of options. For instance, an HR department can likely provide your assessment with literally hundreds of interesting types of data within most any organization (performance appraisals of new hires vs. long-term staff, number of training courses attended by administrative vs. sales staff).

The good news is that all of this affords new perspectives in defining needs (and assets) within an organization, community, or society. Utilizing existing data, you have evidence to support trends that would have been based primarily on assumptions (or limited data) in the past. Likewise, conducting state-wide assessments (or assessments across multiple locations of a multinational organization) is now feasible, based upon broad representation of the populations involved.

Preparing to conduct assessments from big data (and/or real-time data) does take special considerations. The capturing and analysis of such data sets often requires numerous meetings with organizational IT staff and the utilization of specialized software. Similarly, it can be challenging to determine (before expending resources) what data are most useful for guiding your needs assessment. Therefore, you may have to start by analyzing smaller sets of information. You can then use the results to simulate decisions, and thereby to ensure that whatever is collected in the end will really be used in decisions before making large investments.

With these considerations in mind, needs assessments can gain valuable insights from the vast amount of what is now available on a variety of variables within institutions. Take time to explore the options with those who know the data and what they can (and cannot) tell you. Often opportunities to collect real-time data can help you capture current perspectives on needs and assets. This can be especially important in assessments where stakeholders have high turnover, or when external realities (such as market prices for food or housing) shift dramatically on a daily, weekly, or monthly basis.

Geographic Information Systems (GIS)

Systems, like Google Maps, allows for inexpensive mapping of needs, assets, or participant groups. These services can offer helpful visual elements to the analysis and interpretation of data you collect in your assessment. A map illustrating the available homeless shelters in an urban area can be more effective in guiding decisions than multiple tables with text describing the locations. When combined with other forms of infographics, GIS can help in communicating the results of the assessment.

Mobile Technologies

While there are many technologies influencing how we collect and analyze data, cell phone technologies (smartphone apps, SMS surveys, photovoice, and videos) are pushing these trends like few others. For example, the integration of cameras into most cell phones greatly reduces the cost of photovoice data collection. Photovoice allows stakeholders to describe the needs and assessments within their institution or community in a visual manner, providing new insights that survey questions on a scale of 1 to 5 never could. Similarly, photos can be used to document performance issues. In India, as a case in point, cell phone pictures are utilized in combination with GIS technology to document issues around trash collection—with observers reporting issues by taking pictures and sending them to a group site where they are mapped in real time. (For this and other examples see http://www.clearsouthasia.org/resources/mobile-based_technology.pdf)

SMS (or text message) surveys also offer opportunities to collect real-time data. In Latin America, SMS surveys are used to monitor the price of food in relation to household income (see http://go.worldbank.org/KV9LUG0G40). Services such as SurveyMonkey afford survey access via smartphone and through iPhone or Android apps; all afford your assessment new ways to collect data closer to the time of analysis and subsequent decision making.

Social Networking

Social media tools (Facebook, Twitter, Kickstarter, Google+, WeShareScience, and others) are new ways to connect with your stakeholder audiences. From raising funds for your needs assessment (Kickstarter) to getting the word out of stakeholders about opportunities to participate (Twitter), social media tools can be used effectively throughout many assessments.

During the needs assessment, it is often worthwhile to monitor social media since it can work equally for you as against you. While positive

NEW DIRECTIONS FOR EVALUATION • DOI: 10.1002/ev

messages might expand opportunities to reach stakeholders, negative messages from groups with alternative agendas might reduce participation in your assessment. Using free services, you can, search for mentions of key words (e.g., the name of your organization + needs assessment) on major social media sites like Facebook, Reddit, and Twitter.

It should be noted that many of these exciting technology opportunities remain primarily accessible by the most affluent in the world. We must not be blind to the digital divide and should counterbalance technology-driven methods with those that are more equitable for the communities and stakeholders with which you are working. If for budget reasons your primary survey tool is online, then you may have to offset it by holding focus groups in less economically developed parts of the community to ensure that its voice is included in the assessment as well.

Globalization

Needs assessments take place within the context of the world around us. Therefore, globalization continues to affect the development of assessment methods (Sachs, McArthur, & Schmidt-Traub, 2004). Even for a local community- or organization-specific needs assessment, it is of benefit to be aware of how globalization influences our actions. It has significantly increased cultural awareness in terms of who and how we engage with a variety of stakeholder groups. From considerations on how to word survey items to be culturally sensitive to selecting appropriate focus group facilitators for different audiences, the changing diversity in workplaces and communities means that we must be keenly aware of our actions. After all, you would not want your assessment results to be skewed because of an unintentional oversight that led to important stakeholders not participating. Any needs assessment must resonate with the cultures and backgrounds of those who will implement the activities that follow. This is as true in Indiana as it is in India.

With these considerations in mind, new methods have evolved to help assessors. Participatory methods (affected by parallel work in evaluation) are now common in many assessments. Similarly, new models for needs assessment (including the hybrid approach described in Chapter 7 of this issue) also strengthen the inclusion of diverse stakeholder groups into the assessment process.

Globalization has brought with it renewed interest in cross-disciplinary applications of needs assessment. From community psychology, medicine, and business to education and international development, we now find collaborations on assessments that span traditional boundaries. This is not to say that all assessments should cross fields or disciplines; many do not for very practical reasons. But we are learning from other disciplines to improve our theories, models, and methods. This cross-fertilization often happens in very practical ways (a needs assessment done in a business is shared by email with a community psychologist without much fanfare). And these small events lead to new techniques being tried out and new theories being developed.

It is an exciting time to be working in the field of needs assessment. Technology, globalization, and new methods make the identification and prioritization of needs better and more impactful. Nevertheless, these trends can at times obscure, hide, or even amplify some of the methodological challenges that professionals assessing needs have confronted for years. As a result, it is critical that we pay closer attention to the validity of our methods as these trends continue to shape our research and practice.

Concerns

Amid the excitement of 21st century needs assessment, we must highlight a few of the concerns that should guide our future research and practice. One is at the core of needs assessment theory and practice, and is derived specifically from how we define and therefore measure needs. The common discrepancy definition of needs is practical on many levels, but its measurement can lead to issues that influence recommendations coming from an assessment. On the surface, needs assessment seems very simple—ask about what should be (desired) and what is (current) status and then compare one to the other to see if a need is there. A higher desired score than the one for the current condition is the discrepancy indicator, and the larger the discrepancy, the greater the need. Yet there are many complications. For instance, we commonly subtract two related scales (desired − current = need), each with inherent measurement error in it. Difference scores compound error and may lead to unreliable results with limited or specious utility.

If on a survey, for example, you measure the desired results on a scale of 1 to 6, with 1 equaling "not important" and 6 equaling "very important," you will naturally get some measurement error since individual participants may interpret the scale differently (a 4 for you may be a 5 for me). Add to this the fact that we don't know the rationale for why an item is rated the way it is by respondents (is it based on accurate knowledge of an area, limited knowledge, or perhaps no knowledge whatsoever?), and you could find that you have a fair amount of uncertainty within the survey.

White and Altschuld (2012) explored the meaning of the "what should be" scores given by respondents and came to the conclusion that they are difficult to interpret without more understanding of what underlies them. When we factor in that in many instances Don't Know (DK) or Not Applicable (NA) choices were not available, it gets harder to interpret data.

Additionally, if you then compare what should be with what is data, where 1 equals "never" and 6 equals "always," you add to the problem. Subtracting a "frequency" rating (for what is) from an "importance" (for desired) would not be responsible. It is quite challenging to write needs

Table 8.1. Sampling of Methodological Concerns

Concern	What Should Be	What Is	Comments
Double or multiple scaled forms	Meaningfully worded scales permitting appropriate subtraction between scales	Frequent use of multiple scales without required attention to wording	Can lead to erroneous conclusions about needs; better wording somewhat reduces the problem
Not Applicable (NA) or Don't Know (DK) responses	Increased usage of such options allows for clearer interpretation of data	Not employed as frequently as they should be	Can allow surveyors to get a more realistic perspective of the respondents and the basis for their replies
Analysis of multiple scaled forms	Weighted needs indices, proportionate reduction in error, means difference analysis, and other approaches	Simple item-by-item mean subtractions with inherent problems predicated on less-than-optimum wording and compounded error	Sophisticated procedures for analysis are warranted in order to properly inform decisions
Ways to portray data from multiple sources	Straightforward and utilitarian formats for information that facilitate decision making	Some discussion of this in the literature and in reports, though not taking into account when results do not agree	Not enough emphasis given on how to array, summarize, and integrate their results
Research about the assessment of needs	Robust study of methods and approaches for looking at needs (i.e., NA as a research area)	Research is done but falls short of what is required to guide practice	With research-based practice, the quality of assessments should be enhanced; practitioners should review literature as they go about assessing needs
Evaluation of the enterprise itself	Needs assessments should be evaluated formatively and in a summative fashion for outcomes	Hardly any evaluations are reported, some for joint needs assessments and asset capacity building endeavors	We must evaluate what we are doing and whether it has produced positive change and growth; we should be learning from what did and did not work

Figure 8.1. Examples of Data-Collection Tools and Techniques for Each Data Type (Watkins, 2007; Watkins, West Meiers, & Visser, 2012)

	Hard (externally verifiable data)	Soft (not externally verifiable data)
Quantitative (numeric expressions of a variable)	• Performance data • Budget analysis	• Performance ratings • Scaled surveys (e.g., 1= disagree, 5= agree)
Qualitative (non- numeric expressions of a variable)	• Analysis of a list serve • Document review • Focus groups • Multisource performance observations	• Opinion surveys • Individual interviews • Single source performance observations

assessment questions that measure desired and current results on equivalent scales. We must be aware of (and forthright about) measurement problems and error when we design, implement, report, and make recommendations.

Table 8.1 contains an overview of some of the concerns that commonly occur in needs assessment studies (there could be more entries). The purpose here is to sensitize you to the challenges we have as assessors and to the vast possibilities for research into the field.

As a result of these concerns, rarely should you rely on one measurement method (e.g., survey or focus group) alone to identify needs. Cross-validate your findings with a mix of *hard* (externally verifiable) and *soft* (not externally verifiable) methods, as well as *qualitative* (words) and *quantitative* (numbers) methods (see Figure 8.1). And when you report on results, align them to data sources so that accurate comparisons and contrasts can be made. These improvements to how we collect and analyze data will become all the more critical as we use new technologies (discussed above) to broaden our use of data to drive assessment findings and recommendations.

Summary

Obviously, many more issues could have been included, such as translation of items and scales across cultures, assessor subjectivity or bias, and response rates. We encourage you to conduct "action research" in your assessments or design investigations that could help make collecting data about needs and methods used substantially better. It is only by those of us engaged in assessment activities working to improve our methods that substantial gains in the validity and reliability of assessment can be made in the coming years. And if possible, write up what you have done and submit it for publication. People who have done so have improved the work in needs assessment and we are all grateful for such efforts.

As a field of practice (rather than a field of "pure" research), we do recognize that many of the valuable improvements in methods may not come through traditional academic research and publications. We have therefore created a repository (NA Docs) on the www.NeedsAssessment.org website for sharing tools and techniques (as well as research) that can help all of us improve our methods. These will not be vetted, as peer-reviewed research articles would be, but we hope that by sharing resources in common place where practitioners and researchers can collaborate, everyone can improve in needs assessment practice over time.

References

Altschuld, J. W. (Ed.). (2010). *The needs assessment kit.* Thousand Oaks, CA: Sage.

Altschuld, J. W., & White, J. L. (2010). *The needs assessment kit—Analysis and prioritization* (Book 4). Thousand Oaks, CA: Sage.

Kamis, E. (1979). A witness for the defense of needs assessment. *Evaluation and Program Planning, 2,* 7–12.

Kaufman, R., Guerra-Lopez, I., Watkins, R., & Leigh, D. (2008). *The assessment book: Applied strategic thinking and performance improvement through self-assessments.* Amherst, MA: HRD Press.

Leigh, D. (2009). SWOT analysis. In R. Watkins & D. Leigh (Eds.), *The handbook of improving performance in the workplace, Volume 2: Selecting and implementing performance interventions* (pp. 115–140). San Francisco, CA: Wiley.

Sachs, J., McArthur, J., & Schmidt-Traub, G (2004). *Millennium development goals needs assessments: Country case studies of Bangladesh, Cambodia, Ghana, Tanzania and Uganda.* New York, NY: United Nations. Retrieved from http://www.unmillenniumproject.org/documents/mp_ccspaper_jan1704.pdf

Watkins, R. (2007). *Performance by design: The systematic selection, design, and development of performance technologies that produce useful results.* Amherst, MA: HRD Press.

Watkins, R., West Meiers, M., & Visser, Y. (2012). *A guide to assessing needs: Tools for collecting information, making decisions, and achieving development results.* Washington, DC: World Bank.

Weisbord, M., & Janoff, S. (2009). Future search. In R. Watkins & D. Leigh (Eds.), *The handbook of improving performance in the workplace, Volume 2: Selecting and implementing performance interventions* (pp. 91–114). San Francisco, CA: Wiley.

White, J., & Altschuld, J. (2012). Understanding the "What Should Be Condition" in needs assessment data. *Evaluation and Program Planning, 35*(1), 124–132.

Witkin, B. R. (1994). Needs assessment since 1981: The state of practice. *Evaluation Practice, 15*(1), 17–27.

RYAN WATKINS *is an associate professor at George Washington University in Washington, DC, and founder of www.NeedsAssessment.org and www.WeShareScience.com.*

JAMES W. ALTSCHULD *is professor emeritus in the College of Education and Human Ecology, The Ohio State University.*

NEW DIRECTIONS FOR EVALUATION • DOI: 10.1002/ev

INDEX